Cadillac Automobiles 1960-1969

Compiled by
R.M. Clarke

ISBN 1 869826 809

Booklands Books Ltd.
PO Box 146, Cobham, KT11 1LG
Surrey, England

Printed in Hong Kong

BROOKLANDS BOOKS

BROOKLANDS ROAD TEST SERIES

AC Ace & Aceca 1953-1983
Alfa Romeo Alfasud 1972-1984
Alfa Romeo Alfetta Coupes GT. GTV. GTV6 1974-1987
Alfa Romeo Giulia Berlinas 1962-1976
Alfa Romeo Giulia Coupes Gold Portfolio 1963-1976
Alfa Romeo Giulia Coupes 1963-1976
Alfa Romeo Giulietta Gold Portfolio 1954-1965
Alfa Romeo Spider Gold Portfolio 1966-1991
Alfa Romeo Spider 1966-1990
Allard Gold Portfolio 1937-1959
Alvis Gold Portfolio 1919-1967
American Motors Muscle Cars 1966-1970
Armstrong Siddeley Gold Portfolio 1945-1960
Aston Martin Gold Portfolio 1972-1985
Austin Seven 1922-1982
Austin A30 & A35 1951-1962
Austin Healey 100 & 100/6 Gold Portfolio 1952-1959
Austin Healey 3000 Gold Portfolio 1959-1967
Austin Healey Sprite 1958-1971
Avanti 1962-1990
BMW Six Cylinder Coupes 1969-1975
BMW 1600 Col. 1 1966-1981
BMW 2002 1968-1976
BMW 316, 318, 320 Gold Portfolio 1975-1990
BMW 320, 323, 325 Gold Portfolio 1977-1990
Buick Automobiles 1947-1960
Buick Muscle Cars 1965-1970
Buick Riviera 1963-1978
Cadillac Automobiles 1949-1959
Cadillac Automobiles 1960-1969
Cadillac Eldorado 1967-1978
High Performance Capris Gold Portfolio 1969-1987
Chevrolet Camaro SS & Z28 1966-1973
Chevrolet Camaro & Z-28 1973-1981
High Performance Camaros 1982-1988
Camaro Muscle Portfolio 1967-1973
Chevrolet 1955-1957
Chevrolet Corvair 1959-1969
Chevrolet Impala & SS 1958-1971
Chevrolet Muscle Cars 1966-1971
Chevelle and SS 1964-1972
Chevy Blazer 1969-1981
Chevy EL Camino & SS 1959-1987
Chevy II Nova & SS 1962-1973
Chrysler 300 Gold Portfolio 1955-1970
Citroen Traction Avant Gold Portfolio 1934-1957
Citroen DS & ID 1955-1975
Citroen SM 1970-1975
Citroen 2CV 1949-1988
Shelby Cobra Gold Portfolio 1962-1969
Cobras and Cobra Replicas Gold Portfolio 1962-1989
Cobras & Replicas 1962-1983
Chevrolet Corvette Gold Portfolio 1953 1962
Corvette Stingray Gold Portfolio 1963-1967
Chevrolet Corvettee Gold Portfolio 1968-1977
High Performance Corvettes 1983-1989
Daimler SP250 Sport & V-8250 Saloon Gold Portfolio 1959-1969
Datsun 240Z 1970-1973
Datsun 280Z & ZX 1975-1983
De Tomaso Collection No.1 1962-1981
Dodge Charger 1966-1974
Dodge Muscle Cars 1967-1970
Excalibur Collection No.1 1952-1981
Facel Vega 1954-1964
Ferrari Cars 1946-1956
Ferrari Dino 1965-1974
Ferrari Dino 308 1974-1979
Ferrari 308 & Mondial 1980-1984
Ferrari Collection No.1 1960-1970
Fiat-Bertone X1/9 1973-1988
Fiat Pininfarina 124 + 2000 Spider 1968-1985
Ford Automobiles 1949-1959
Ford Bronco 1966-1977
Ford Bronco 1978-1988
Ford Consul. Zephyr Zodiac MkI & II 1950-1962
Ford Cortina 1600E & GT 1967-1970
Ford Fairlane 1955-1970
Ford Falcon 1960-1970
Ford GT40 Gold Portfolio 1964-1987
Ford RS Escorts 1968-1980
Ford Zephyr Zodiac Executive MkIII & MkIV 1962-1971
High Performance Capris Gold Portfolio 1969-1987
High Performance Escorts Mk1 1968-1974
High Performance Escorts Mk II 1975-1980
High Performance Escorts 1980-1985
High Performance Escorts 1985-1990
High Performance Fiestas 1979-1991
High Performance Mustangs 1982-1988
Holden 1948-1962
Honda CRX 1983-1987
Hudson & Railton 1936-1940
Jaguar and SS Gold Portfolio 1931-1951
Jaguar XK120 XK140 XK150 Gold Portfolio 1948-1960
Jaguar MkVII VIII IX X 420 Gold Portfolio 1950-1970
Jaguar Cars 1961-1964
Jaguar Mk2 1959-1969
Jaguar E-Type Gold Portfolio 1961-1971
Jaguar E-Type 1966-1971
Jaguar E-Type V-12 1971-1975
Jaguar XJ12 XJ5.3 V12 Glold Portfolio 1972-1990
Jaguar XJ6 Series II 1973-1979
Jaguar XJ6 Series III 1979-1986
Jaguar XJS Gold Portfolio 1975-1990
Jeep CJ5 & CJ6 1960-1976
Jeep CJ5 & CJ7 1976-1986
Jensen Cars 1946-1967
Jensen Cars 1967-1979
Jensen Interceptor Gold Portfolio 1966-1986
Jensen Healey 1972-1976
Lamborghini Cars 1964-1970
Lamborghini Countach Col No.1 1971-1982
Lamborghini Countach & Urraco 1974-1980
Lamborghini Countach & Jalpa 1980-1985
Lancia Stratos 1972-1985
Land Rover Series I 1948-1958
Land Rover Series II & IIa 1958-1971
Land Rover Series III 1971-1985
Land Rover 90 & 110 1983-1989
Lincoln Gold Portfolio 1949-1960
Lincoln Continental 1961-1969
Lincoln Continental 1969-1976
Lotus and Caterham Seven Gold Portfolio 1957-1989
Lotus Cortina Gold Portfolio 1963-1970
Lotus Elan Gold Portfolio 1962-1974
Lotus Elan Collection No.2 1963-1972
Lotus Elite 1957-1964
Lotus Elite & Eclat 1974-1982
Lotus Turbo Esprit 1980-1986
Lotus Europa Gold Portfolio 1966-1975
Marcos Cars 1960-1988
Maserati 1965-1970
Maserati 1970-1975
Mazda RX-7 Collection No.1 1978-1981
Mercedes 190 & 300SL 1954-1963
Mercedes 230/250/280SL 1963-1971
Mercedes Benz SLs & SLCs Gold Portfolio 1971-1989
Mercedes Benz Cars 1949-1954
Mercedes Benz Cars 1954-1957
Mercedes Benz Cars 1957-1961
Mercedes Benz Competion Cars 1950-1957
Mercury Muscle Cars 1966-1971
Metropolitan 1954-1962
MG TC 1945-1949
MG TD 1949-1953
MG TF 1953-1955
MG Cars 1959-1962
MGA & Twin Cam Gold Portfolio 1955-1962
MGB MGC & V8 Gold Portfolio 1962-1980
MGB Roadsters 1962-1980
MGB GT 1965-1980
MG Midget 1961-1980
Mini Cooper Gold Portfolio 1961-1971
Mini Moke 1964-1989
Mini Muscle Cars 1961-1979
Mopar Muscle Cars 1964-1967
Morgan Three-Wheeler Gold Portfolio 1910-1952
Morgan Cars 1960-1970
Morgan Cars Gold Portfolio 1968-1989
Morris Minor Collection No.1
Mustang Muscle Cars 1967-1971
Oldsmobile Automobiles 1955-1963
Old's Cutlass & 4-4-2 1964-1972
Oldsmobile Muscle Cars 1964-1971
Oldsmobile Toronado 1966-1978
Opel GT 1968-1973
Packard Gold Portfolio 1946-1958
Pantera Gold Portfolio 1970-1989
Panther Gold Portfolio 1972-1990
Plymouth Barracuda 1964-1974
Plymouth Muscle Cars 1966-1971
Pontiac Tempest & GTO 1961-1965
Pontiac Firebird and Trans-Am 1973-1981
High Performance Firebirds 1982-1988
Pontiac Fiero 1984-1988
Pontiac Muscle Cars 1966-1972
Porsche 356 1952-1965
Porsche Cars in the 60's
Porsche Cars 1960-1964
Porsche Cars 1964-1968
Porsche Cars 1968-1972
Porsche Cars 1972-1975
Porsche Turbo Collection No.1 1975-1980
Porsche 911 1965-1969
Porsche 911 1970-1972
Porsche 911 1973-1977
Porsche 911 Carrera 1973-1977
Porsche 911 Turbo 1975-1984
Porsche 911 SC 1978-1983
Porsche 914 Gold Portfolio 1969-1976
Porsche 914 Collection No.1 1969-1983
Porsche 924 Gold Portfolio 1975-1988
Porsche 928 1977-1989
Porsche 944 1981-1985
Range Rover Gold Portfolio 1970-1988
Reliant Scimitar 1964-1986
Riley 11/2 & 21/2 Litre Gold Portfolio 1945-1955
Rolls Royce Silver Cloud Gold Portfolio 1955-1965
Rolls Royce Silver Shadow 1965-1981
Rover P4 1949-1959
Rover P4 1955-1964
Rover 3 & 3.5 Litre Gold Portfolio 1958-1973
Rover 2000 + 2200 1963-1977
Rover 3500 1968-1977
Rover 3500 & Vitesse 1976-1986
Saab Sonett Collection No.1 1966-1974
Saab Turbo 1976-1983
Shelby Mustang Muscle Portfolio 1965-1970
Stubebaker Gold Portfolio 1947-1966
Stubebaker Hawks & Larks 1956-1963
Sunbeam Tiger & Alpine Gold Portfolio 1959-1967
Thunderbird 1955-1957
Thunderbird 1958-1963
Thunderbird 1964-1976
Toyota Land Cruiser 1956-1984
Toyota MR2 1984-1988
Triumph 2000. 2.5. 2500 1963-1977
Triumph GT6 1966-1974
Triumph Spitfire Gold Portfolio 1962-1980
Triumph Stag 1970-1980
Triumph Stag Collection No.1 1970-1984
Triumph TR2 & TR3 1952-60
Triumph TR4-TR5-TR250 1961-1968
Triumph TR6 Gold Portfolio 1969-1976
Triumph TR7 & TR8 1975-1982
Triumph Herald 1959-1971
Triumph Vitesse 1962-1971
TVR Gold Portfolio 1959-1990
Valiant 1960-1962
VW Beetle Collection No.1 1970-1982
VW Golf GTi 1976-1986
VW Karmann Ghia 1955-1982
VW Kubelwagen 1940-1975
VW Scirocco 1974-1981
VW Bus. Camper. Van 1954-1967
VW Bus. Camper. Van 1968-1979
VW Bus. Camper. Van 1979-1989
Volvo 120 1956-1970
Volvo 1800 Gold Portfolio 1960-1973

BROOKLANDS ROAD & TRACK SERIES

Road & Track on Alfa Romeo 1949-1963
Road & Track on Alfa Romeo 1964-1970
Road & Track on Alfa Romeo 1971-1976
Road & Track on Alfa Romeo 1977-1989
Road & Track on Aston Martin 1962-1990
Road & Track on Auburn Cord and Duesenburg 1952-1984
Road & Track on Audi & Auto Union 1952-1980
Road & Track on Audi 1980-1986
Road & Track on Austin Healey 1953-1970
Road & Track on BMW Cars 1966-1974
Road & Track on BMW Cars 1975-1978
Road & Track on BMW Cars 1979-1983
Road & Track on Cobra, Shelby & GT40 1962-1983
Road & Track on Corvette 1953-1967
Road & Track on Corvette 1968-1982
Road & Track on Corvette 1982-1986
Road & Track on Corvette 1986-1990
Road & Track on Datsun Z 1970-1983
Road & Track on Ferrari 1950-1968
Road & Track on Ferrari 1968-1974
Road & Track on Ferrari 1975-1981
Road & Track on Ferrari 1981-1984
Road & Track on Ferrari 1984-1988
Road & Track on Fiat Sports Cars 1968-1987
Road & Track on Jaguar 1950-1960
Road & Track on Jaguar 1961-1968
Road & Track on Jaguar 1968-1974
Road & Track on Jaguar 1974-1982
Road & Track on Jaguar 1983-1989
Road & Track on Lamborghini 1964-1985
Road & Track on Lotus 1972-1981
Road & Track on Maserati 1952-1974
Road & Track on Maserati 1975-1983
Road & Track on Mazda RX7 1978-1986
Road & Track on Mazda RX7 & MX5 Miata 1986-1991
Road & Track on Mercedes 1952-1962
Road & Track on Mercedes 1963-1970
Road & Track on Mercedes 1971-1979
Road & Track on Mercedes 1980-1987
Road & Track on MG Sports Cars 1949-1961
Road & Track on MG Sprots Cars 1962-1980
Road & Track on Mustang 1964-1977
Road & Track on Nissan 300-ZX & Turbo 1984-1989
Road & Track on Peugeot 1955-1986
Road & Track on Pontiac 1960-1983
Road & Track on Porsche 1961-1967
Road & Track on Porsche 1968-1971
Road & Track on Porsche 1972-1975
Road & Track on Porsche 1975-1978
Road & Track on Porsche 1979-1982
Road & Track on Porsche 1982-1985
Road & Track on Porsche 1985-1988
Road & Track on Rolls Royce & B'ley 1950-1965
Road & Track on Rolls Royce & B'ley 1966-1984
Road & Track on Saab 1955-1985
Road & Track on Toyota Sports & GT Cars 1966-1984
Road & Track on Triumph Sports Cars 1953-1967
Road & Track on Triumph Sports Cars 1967-1974
Road & Track on Triumph Sports Cars 1974-1982
Road & Track on Volkswagen 1951-1968
Road & Track on Volkswagen 1968-1978
Road & Track on Volkswagen 1978-1985
Road & Track on Volvo 1957-1974
Road & Track on Volvo 1975-1985
Road & Track - Henry Manney at Large and Abroad

BROOKLANDS CAR AND DRIVER SERIES

Car and Driver on BMW 1955-1977
Car and Driver on BMW 1977-1985
Car and Driver on Cobra, Shelby & Ford GT 40 1963-1984
Car and Driver on Corvette 1956-1967
Car and Driver on Corvette 1968-1977
Car and Driver on Corvette 1978-1982
Car and Driver on Corvette 1983-1988
Car and Driver on Datsun Z 1600 & 2000 1966-1984
Car and Driver on Ferrari 1955-1962
Car and Driver on Ferrari 1963-1975
Car and Driver on Ferrari 1976-1983
Car and Driver on Mopar 1956-1967
Car and Driver on Mopar 1968-1975
Car and Driver on Mustang 1964-1972
Car and Driver on Pontiac 1961-1975
Car and Driver on Porsche 1955-1962
Car and Driver on Porsche 1963-1970
Car and Driver on Porsche 1970-1976
Car and Driver on Porsche 1977-1981
Car and Driver on Porsche 1982-1986
Car and Driver on Saab 1956-1985
Car and Driver on Volvo 1955-1986

BROOKLANDS PRACTICAL CLASSICS SERIES

PC on Austin A40 Restoration
PC on Land Rover Restoration
PC on Metalworking in Restoration
PC on Midget/Sprite Restoration
PC on Mini Cooper Restoration
PC on MGB Restoration
PC on Morris Minor Restoration
PC on Sunbeam Rapier Restoration
PC on Triumph Herald/Vitesse
PC on Triumph Spitfire Restoration
PC on VW Beetle Restoration
PC on 1930s Car Restoration

BROOKLANDS HOT ROD 'MUSCLECAR & HI-PO ENGINE SERIES

Chevy 265 & 283
Chevy 302 & 327
Chevy 348 & 409
Chevy 350 & 400
Chevy 396 & 427
Chevy 454 thru 512
Chrysler Hemi
Chrysler 273, 318, 340 & 360
Chrysler 361, 383, 400, 413, 426, 440
Ford 289, 302, Boss 302 & 351W
Ford 351C & Boss 351
Ford Big Block

BROOKLANDS MILITARY VEHICLES SERIES

Allied Mil. Vehicles No.1 1942-1945
Allied Mil. Vehicles No.2 1941-1946
Dodge Mil. Vehicles Col. 1 1940-1945
Military Jeeps 1941-1945
Off Road Jeeps 1944-1971
Hail to the Jeep
Complete WW2 Military Jeep Manual
US Military Vehicles 1941-1945
US Army Military Vehicles WW2-TM9-2800

BROOKLANDS HOT ROD RESTORATION SERIES

Auto Restoration Tips & Techniques
Basic Bodywork Tips & Techniques
Basic Painting Tips & Techniques
Camaro Restoration Tips & Techniques
Chevrolet High Performance Tips & Techniques
Chevy-GMC Pickup Repair
Custom Painting Tips & Techniques
Engine Swapping Tips & Techniques
Ford Pickup Repair
How to Build a Street Rod
Mustang Restoration Tips & Techniques
Performance Tuning - Chevrolets of the '60s
Performance Tuning - Ford of the '60s
Performance Tuning - Mopars of the '60s
Performance Tuning - Pontiacs of the '60s

CONTENTS

Page	Title	Publication	Date	Year
5	Testing the Luxury Cars — Comparison Test	Motor Life	Aug.	1960
10	Cadillac — 1961	Motor Trend	Nov.	1960
12	1961 Cadillac Engineering	Automobile Topics	Dec.	1960
13	Cadillac — A New Trend to Conservative Luxury	Motor Trend	April	1961
16	Return of Cadillac	Wheels	April	1961
18	Three for the Money	Motor Life	July	1961
22	60th Anniversary Cadillacs	Automobile Topics	Oct.	1961
23	Egad — A Cad! Road Test	Modern Motor	Jan.	1962
26	Cadillac — Imperial — Lincoln Road Test	Motor Trend	May	1962
34	Caddy Produces New Engine	Popular Science	Nov.	1962
35	Cadillac Gets Lighter Engine	Popular Mechanics	Nov.	1962
37	Introducing the '63 Cadillac	Car Life	Nov.	1962
38	Cadillac Cross-Country Road Test	Motor Trend	Jan.	1963
44	Cadillac Owners Report	Popular Mechanics	June	1963
47	'64 Cadillac Makes Its Own Weather	Popular Mechanics	June	1963
48	Cadillac Series 60	Car Life	Nov.	1963
50	Cadillac Sedan de Ville Road Test	Motor Trend	March	1964
56	Cadillac Sedan de Ville Road Test	Car Life	July	1964
60	The 1965 Cadillacs	Car and Driver	Oct.	1964
61	Six Luxury Cars — A Subjective Evaluation	Car and Driver	July	1965
74	GM's Crown Jewel	Motor Trend	Aug.	1965
78	Cadillac Range and Specifications	Motor Trend Yearbook		1966
80	Go West Young Man . . . Sedan de Ville	Motor Trend	Jan.	1966
84	Cadillac Owners Claim You Get a Lot to Like	Popular Mechanics	July	1966
86	Cadillac for 1967	Car Life	Nov.	1966
87	Cadillac 1968 — Mini Tests	Car and Driver	Dec.	1967
88	Arrival of the Fittest — Comparison Test	Motor Trend	April	1969
95	Cadillac Coupe de Ville Road Test	Road Test	May	1969

ACKNOWLEDGEMENTS

This is our fourth book on Cadillac and it might be useful here to explain how we are historically covering the products of this prestigious company.

Our first book Cadillac in the Sixties — No. 1 was a 72 page international collection of stories which sketchily reported on the main models of the decade, and was produced primarily to see how strong interest was in the marque.

We followed this with the 100 page — Cadillac Eldorado 1967-1978 which dealt solely and in depth with the advanced front-wheel-drive machines that were unveiled late in 1966.

A strong plea from friends in Sweden for information on earlier models sent us to the archives once again, the outcome being — Cadillac Automobiles 1949-1959. This book is biased towards the heavily finned 1957/1959 models which are now so sought after by collectors.

Our reason for returning to the sixties with this book is that we now know that there is a keen following for the luxury cars of the period, which from a US viewpoint was dominated by Cadillac. In order to paint an overall picture we have included pieces on other leading makes by incorporating a number of comparison tests and reports. These illustrate where Cadillac was positioned technically and saleswise in the marketplace with regard to their main competitors — Lincoln and Chrysler and to a lesser extent to Mercedes with their formidable 600 limousine. We have deliberately excluded the fwd Eldorado's as they have been dealt with elsewhere and we have been careful not to duplicate any of the stories from earlier volumes.

Our books are printed in small numbers and now with over 300 titles are one of the main reference works for those that indulge in the hobby of automobile restoration. We exist because firstly there is a need by enthusiasts for this information and secondly because the publishers of the world's leading motoring journals generously support us by allowing us to include their copyright articles. We are indebted in this instance to the management of Automobile Topics, Car and Driver, Car Life, Modern Motor, Motor Life, Motor Trend, Popular Mechanics, Popular Science, Road Test and Wheels for their ongoing support.

R.M. Clarke

TESTING THE Luxury CARS

Checking the big ones – from their polite performance to their gorgeous gadgets

FOR SHEER luxury, Detroit provides three magnificent choices, Cadillac, Imperial and Lincoln. No other car in this country and a few from overseas can equal the refinement of these.

Perhaps the best way to characterize the three is in contrast to another car in the same price class, the Chrysler 300-F. It, too, is refined but in an entirely different way. It has been engineered to put the driver in intimate touch with the machine and the machine with the road. By luxury car standards, it has rough, noisy operation.

Cadillac, Imperial and Lincoln are just the reverse. Everything about them isolates their occupants from the road; the whole emphasis is on smoothness and silence. This, as the tests reveal, has its effects on their merits as automobiles.

Each of the three is a different solution to the problem of including a luxury car within a broad corporate line. Cadillac shares its body shell with other General Motors makes but has its own engine and chassis. Imperial and Lincoln follow an opposite policy, using the same mechanical components as their medium-priced running mates with their own distinctive structures. And distinctive they are. Imperial is Chrysler's sole product with a separate body and frame while Lincoln is Ford's only full-sized car with unit construction.

In their regular lines, each offers three series. Cadillac has the 62, Fleetwood 60 Special and Eldorado, Imperial the Custom, Crown and Le Baron and Lincoln the plain Lincoln, Premiere and Continental Mark V. Prices range from $4892 to $7401 for Cadillac, $4922 to $6318 for Imperial and $5252 to $7056 for Lincoln.

All of the closed Cadillacs are hardtops while Imperial and Lincoln each use the same bodies and charge the same prices for four-door sedans and hardtops.

They all build formal cars as well, Cadillac the 75 eight-passenger sedan and limousine costing up to $9748, Imperial the eight-passenger Crown limousine at $15,600 and Lincoln the six-passenger Continental town car and limousine reaching $10,230.

Finally, Cadillac has the Eldorado Brougham at $13,075. Both the Brougham and Imperial limousine have bodies built in Italy so the Lincoln Continental limousine is left with the title of the most expensive car made in this country.

Turning from high finance, the cars actually tested for this report were a Cadillac 62, Imperial Le Baron and Lincoln Continental. Strictly speaking, Cadillac's equivalent to the Le Baron and Continental is the Fleetwood 60 Special but, because the 60 and 62 are the same mechanically, the test results are still comparable.

In every other respect, the three cars were similar. All were four-door hardtops with complete power equipment and air conditioning to equalize any weight advantages. It would have been difficult to have them unlike because so many accessories, power steering, power brakes and automatic transmissions as well as minor niceties like electric clocks, windshield washers, remote control outside mirrors and back-up lights, are all standard. Lincoln goes all the way and even includes radios and heaters at no extra cost.

This may well be a last look at the high-priced field as it has long existed. Just as the Rambler has revolutionized popular car concepts, the Thunderbird has pointed the way to new ideas in luxury. Specifically, it has dispelled the notion that a relatively expensive car must be big.

CADILLAC

For 1960, Cadillac continues the basic design introduced last year with important changes in its suspension and braking systems.

It proved the best performer of the trio, even though it had the smallest engine. From 0-to-60, the 62 test car averaged 10.7 seconds, beating the Imperial and Lincoln by 1.6 and 3.5 seconds, respectively.

The 390-cubic-inch engine is essentially an enlarged version of the first ohv V-8 offered by Cadillac 11 years ago. It develops 325 hp with 10.5-to-1 compression and single four-barrel carbure-

CADILLAC interior is least ornate of the tested trio, but basic quality and solidity make it most outstanding within this area.

LINCOLN dash is impressive but confusing home of buttons and dials. Driver has trouble just scanning full range of panel.

IMPERIAL instruments are carried out in same massive proportions as rest of car. Some are more for style than function.

TESTING THE LUXURY CARS

tion. For those who want a bit more spirit, there is a 345-hp modification with triple two-barrel carburetion, standard in the Eldorado and optional in other series.

Behind this particular Cadillac's superior acceleration was lower gearing. With air conditioning, the factory installs a 3.21 rear axle ratio instead of the normal 2.94. This, of course, increases fuel consumption; the 62's 10-to-13 mpg range was poorest of the luxury cars.

At first, the 62 does not feel as lively as it really is because engine noise and vibration levels are so low. An important factor here, and a good example of Cadillac's attention to detail, is the radiator fan fitted to air-conditioned cars. It has a temperature-controlled clutch to reduce fan noise at high speeds.

The coil springs, front and rear, have 10 per cent softer rates this year. As a result, riding qualities are smoother but less stable. The car behaves beautifully on even surfaces at moderate speeds. Across dips and around corners, however, it floats and sways badly.

When travelling fast on a narrow country road, proper control is quite difficult. The car seems to feel, literally, all over the road.

Another annoyance, even on well-paved surfaces, is a vibration that occurs between 60 and 70 mph. Apparently it is caused by a point of resonance in the "X" frame because it disappears beyond 70 mph.

The brakes, too, have been altered. They now adjust themselves, taking up any slack when the car is driven in reverse. At the rear, extended and finned drums improve cooling and allow slightly bigger cylinders. Most interesting of all is a new vacuum release for the parking brake. It operates automatically when the engine is running and the car is placed in gear.

This has several advantages. It makes it impossible for the car to be driven with the brake on, it prevents accidental release when the ignition is off and it provides a true emergency brake. Since the parking brake will not lock with the car in gear, it can be used as a supplementary source of stopping power when the car is in motion.

The 62 four-door hardtop, called a Sedan de Ville in its more lavishly trimmed version, comes in two shapes at the same price. One has a flat roof and four side windows, the other a sloping roof and six side windows. The test car was an example of the latter, which seems more practical because it has more interior height, providing space for a higher seat cushion and greater head room in front.

Generally, the Cadillac does not give the impression of being an unusually roomy car, though its interior dimensions compare favorably with those of the Imperial and Lincoln. One difficulty is its awkward entry and exit, hindered in front by the windshield dog leg and in back by a narrow door opening and deep floor wells.

Interior details are very well planned. The instrument panel is recessed to eliminate reflections and includes the shift quadrant. Minor controls and switches all seem out of the way, yet easy to reach. An interesting touch is the removal of the turn indicator lights from the instrument cluster. There is now an amber light in the chrome strip above each front fender that lets the driver know he is signalling for a turn.

But perhaps Cadillac's most impressive feature is its quality. Not just the excellence of finish or the fact things work but the way they work. Take the power windows, for instance. In most cars, they raise and lower with a whirr, then a clunk. In the Cadillac, they operate with only the slightest hum.

The tremendous popularity of the make (Cadillac sells three times as many cars as Imperial and Lincoln combined) causes

CLEVER DESIGN of the Continental's front doors allows air conditioning tunnel to extend to the rear passenger area. It is the best solution thus far offered to this annoying problem.

a low rate of depreciation. This same popularity, however, virtually eliminates the possibility of a discount on the original price, so a Cadillac would not necessarily be the least expensive buy in its class.

A final note: Cadillac is the only one of the three luxury cars available with any mechanical options and even it has very few, the engines and axle ratios mentioned earlier plus air suspension. Other equipment parallels that offered by Imperial and Lincoln and includes an automatic speed device called Cruise Control.

IMPERIAL

Imperial's latest model features extensive restyling of its four-year-old structure but no major changes in its fundamental engineering.

The Imperial engine, most powerful in the luxury class, is the same 350-hp, 413-cubic-inch V-8 used in the Chrysler New Yorker and serves as a basis of the 375-hp unit in the Chrysler 300-F. It has a 10.1-to-1 compression ratio and a single four-barrel carburetor.

The Le Baron recorded a good balance of acceleration and economy for a car of its weight. It averaged 0-to-60 mph runs at 12.3 seconds and fuel consumption between 11 and 14 mpg.

For roadability, the Imperial is at the head of its class. Its suspension system, torsion bars at the front and semi-elliptics at the rear, proves a comfortable ride can be achieved with a definite feel of control. It is smooth on the boulevard yet steady on the highway.

All Chrysler products are noted for their roadability. Throughout the line, their high-speed handling surpasses that of their competitors by a significant margin. However, except for the stiffly sprung 300-F, it is a virtue that lessens as size increases. In other words, an Imperial is not going to keep up with a Plymouth or Dart over a road racing circuit.

But it will stay well ahead of a Cadillac and safely in front of a Lincoln. It has the most stable suspension of any such big, heavy car built today. Float at cruising speeds and sway in corners are both within limits that enable the driver to keep track of the car's placement on the road. If traction weakens in a turn, the classic technique of increased accelerator pressure puts the Imperial right back on course. It responds to correction far more precisely than its two rivals.

This exaggerates a common characteristic of the luxury cars, the ease with which they can be driven faster than intended. Because they operate so quietly, a driver is often startled by the reading on the speedometer. And in the steadier handling Imperial, such a thing is especially true.

All of which makes the Auto Pilot, Imperial's automatic speed device, a most useful accessory. It was the first unit of its kind and, in an improved form for 1960, has become the best.

Basically, it is a governor that can be locked at a pre-selected speed. The original Auto Pilot, together with the present Cadillac Cruise Control and Lincoln Speed Control, had to be re-set manually every time the brakes were applied. The latest version eliminates this slight inconvenience and will re-engage automatically as soon as the car is returned to the desired cruising speed.

Another interesting new feature is an emergency warning light system. With the flip of a switch, all four turn indicators start flashing. The purpose is to make the car visible when it is stopped on dark roads.

Increased emphasis on quality shows up strongly in the 1960 model. For nearly two years, the make has been built in a separate plant where it can be given more careful attention and the policy is beginning to pay off. The new Imperial has the highest quality of any to bear the name in years. It is not yet the equal of Cadillac but, on the basis of the particular cars tested, it seems to have gained an edge over Lincoln.

The four-door hardtop, listed as a Southampton in the Imperial catalog, now shares its shell with the sedan. Aside from the latter's fixed window frames on the doors, there is no real

MOTOR LIFE TEST DATA

1960 CADILLAC

Test Car

Test Car: Cadillac 62
Body Type: Four-door hardtop
Base Price: $5498

Maneuverability Factors

Overall Length: 225 inches
Overall Width: 79.9 inches
Overall Height: 56.2 inches
Wheelbase: 130 inches
Tread, Front/Rear: 61 and 61 inches
Test Weight: 5130 lbs.
Weight Distribution: 54 per cent on front wheels
Steering: 4 turns lock-to-lock
Turning Circle: 47.8 feet curb-to-curb
Ground Clearance: 5.9 inches

Interior Room

Seating Capacity: Six
Front Seat
 Headroom: 34.2 inches
 Width: 61.7 inches
 Legroom: 45.9 inches
Trunk Capacity: 16.4 cubic feet

Engine & Drive Train

Type: ohv V-8
Displacement: 390 cubic inches
Bore & Stroke: 4.0 x 3.875
Compression Ratio: 10.5-to-1
Carburetion: Single four-barrel
Horsepower: 325 @ 4800 rpm
Torque: 430 lbs-ft @ 3100 rpm
Transmission: Four-speed automatic
Rear Axle Ratio: 3.21

Performance

Gas Mileage: 10 to 13 miles per gallon
Acceleration: 0-30 mph in 4.0 seconds, 0-45 mph in 6.6 seconds and 0-60 mph in 10.7 seconds
Speedometer Error: Indicated 30, 45 and 60 mph are actual 28, 42 and 57 mph respectively
Power-Weight Ratio: 15.8 lbs. per horsepower
Horsepower Per Cubic Inch: .83

MOTOR LIFE TEST DATA

1960 IMPERIAL

Test Car

Test Car: Imperial Le Baron
Body Type: Four-door hardtop
Base Price: $6318

Maneuverability Factors

Overall Length: 226.3 inches
Overall Width: 80.5 inches
Overall Height: 56.7 inches
Wheelbase: 129 inches
Tread, Front/Rear: 61.8 and 62.2 inches
Test Weight: 5260 lbs.
Weight Distribution: 54 per cent on front wheels
Steering: 3.5 turns lock-to-lock
Turning Circle: 48.2 feet curb-to-curb
Ground Clearance: 5.6 inches

Interior Room

Seating Capacity: Six
Front Seat
    Headroom: 34.4 inches
    Width: 61.0 inches
    Legroom: 46.9 inches
Trunk Capacity: 17.8 cubic feet

Engine & Drive Train

Type: ohv V-8
Displacement: 413 cubic inches
Bore & Stroke: 4.18 x 3.75
Compression Ratio: 10.1-to-1
Carburetion: Single four-barrel
Horsepower: 350 @ 4600 rpm
Torque: 470 lbs-ft @ 2800 rpm
Transmission: Three-speed automatic
Rear Axle Ratio: 2.93

Performance

Gas Mileage: 11 to 14 miles per gallon
Acceleration: 0-30 mph in 4.3 seconds, 0-45 mph in 7.3 seconds and 0-60 mph in 12.3 seconds
Speedometer Error: Indicated 30, 45 and 60 mph are actual 30, 44 and 57 mph respectively
Power-Weight Ratio: 15.2 lbs. per horsepower
Horsepower Per Cubic Inch: .85

---

difference between the two. Previously, a different four-door, six-window sedan had been available.

A unique feature of all Imperial body styles is curved glass for the side windows. The Le Baron has the further distinction of an unusually small window, creating an effect of privacy for rear seat passengers but restricting visibility for the driver. He has to be extra cautious about things behind him. Fortunately, the fins and taillights are within his view and serve as some guide when reversing the car.

Two circular dash housings contain a complete set of instruments, including generator, temperature and oil pressure gauges. Thanks to non-glare electroluminescent lighting, they are even easier to read at night than during the day.

Placement of some controls seems to have been dictated by styling rather than function. A particularly irritating case in point is the turn indicator switch. It is on the dash, just to the left of the instrument cluster, where it neatly balances the appearance of the heater lever at the right. However, it is quite awkward to reach. A subtle touch of symmetry hardly seems worth making a frequently-used control less accessible.

Other features for 1960 include the square steering wheel also used by Plymouth and the high-backed driver's seat now offered on all full-sized Chrysler products, both items which have been discussed in earlier tests. And Imperial has finally caught up with Cadillac and Lincoln in another detail; power vent windows have been made available as an option.

LINCOLN

Lincoln has carried its current design into a third year with reduced power and new rear springing.

Its engine has the biggest displacement, 430 cubic inches, and now the lowest output, 315 hp, of the luxury cars. A change from four-barrel to two-barrel carburetion accounts for the drop from last year's 350 hp. The compression ratio remains the same at 10-to-1. Variations of the Lincoln engine power the 310-hp Mercury and the 350-hp Thunderbird.

With a 2.89 rear axle ratio, the Continental Mark V test car was good for no better an average 0-to-60 time than 14.2 seconds. This is the slowest figure recorded this year by any V-8, regardless of price or power. Economy was on a par with Imperial's at 11 to 14 mpg, leading one to wonder why Lincoln did not

VENTILATION of the Lincoln is greatly improved by the rolldown rear window. Driver controls the power operation from his seat. The glass slides into the area behind the rear seat.

challenge the big Chrysler product in the Mobil Economy Run. It was the only make not entered in the 1960 event yet seems capable of a very good showing.

The rear suspension of the 1960 Lincoln is completely new. Previously, coil springs were used but these have been replaced by conventional semi-elliptics. The coil system had been designed so that air suspension could be installed with a minimum of difficulty. However, the option is no longer available.

With the same spring rates, the ride is just as smooth and much steadier. The car does not squat as badly as it did under hard acceleration nor does it dive as sharply when the brakes are applied. There is still some float at high speed but considerably less than there used to be.

In corners, the new Lincoln handles better, though it is still no match for the Imperial. Tires squealing and body leaning, it tends to plow through turns because of its nose heaviness. Approximately 57 per cent of the weight is on the front end.

A redeeming factor, though, is the steering. It is one of the best power-assisted units available. It has enough road feel to please the skilled driver and is remarkably quick. In normal driving, it is even faster than its 3.2 turns lock-to-lock might indicate because the car has a smaller turning circle than either Cadillac or Imperial.

Under traffic conditions, the Linclon is surprisingly easy to maneuver for a car of its size. Crisp fender lines make it less difficult to place in crowded situations than its competitors.

All this is despite its immense bulk. It is the longest, heaviest (and costliest) six-passenger sedan built in this country. It is within an inch of being 19 feet long and has a shipping weight over 5,000 lbs. As tested, it was the heavyweight champion of the year at 5300 lbs.

Interior dimensions are consistent with its overall size. Lincoln has higher seat cushions and more head room, front and rear, than either Cadillac or Imperial. Much of this can be attributed to its unit construction, which allows a greater distance between ceiling and floor because no thick frame members take up space under the passenger's feet.

When the body and frame are combined, a car can become more subject to noise and vibration from road shock. Lincoln has avoided this problem with thorough insulation. Even on the roughest surfaces, it is a quiet car. The Continental tested did have some wind noise at high speeds but this was due simply to an ineffective window seal.

Lincoln calls its four-door hardtop a Landau and, like Imperial, uses the same shell for its sedan.

The Continental series has an exclusive roll-down rear window controlled from a console in the driver's arm rest. The glass slides immediately behind the rear seat so there is no room for a rear radio speaker but it provides wonderful ventilation. On all but the hottest days, it is more pleasant to leave the air conditioning off and lower all the windows to enjoy the forced breeze that comes through the car.

Turning to the dash, instruments and controls are gathered together on a single, flat panel in front of the driver. Heating, ventilating, defrosting and air conditioning are all combined in one of the simplest, easiest arrangements possible. A single knob controls fan level and a dial setting for the kind and temperature of air wanted.

The parking brake has a vacuum release, similar to Cadillac's, that will not function unless the engine is running. However, it is operated by a pushbutton rather than by placing the shift lever in gear.

Two small features will appeal to the family man. The electric door switch is on the dash, right below a red light that goes on if any door is unlocked. Thus, if a child unlocks a rear door, which he must do before he can open it, the driver is immediately warned and can relock it with the dash switch. And the master control for the power windows has a control that cancels operation of all but the windows in the driver's door, preventing small hands from playing with them. ●

MOTOR LIFE TEST DATA

1960 LINCOLN

Test Car

Test Car: Lincoln Continental
Body Type: Four-door hardtop
Base Price: $6845

Maneuverability Factors

Overall Length: 227.2 inches
Overall Width: 80.3 inches
Overall Height: 56.7 inches
Wheelbase: 131 inches
Tread, Front/Rear: 61 and 61 inches
Test Weight: 5300 lbs.
Weight Distribution: 57 per cent on front wheels
Steering: 3.2 turns lock-to-lock
Turning Circle: 45 feet curb-to-curb
Ground Clearance: 6 inches

Interior Room

Seating Capacity: Six
Front Seat
　Headroom: 34.9 inches
　Width: 60.4 inches
　Legroom: 44.0 inches
Trunk Capacity: 17.2 cubic feet

Engine & Drive Train

Type: ohv V-8
Displacement: 430 cubic inches
Bore & Stroke: 4.3 x 3.7
Compression Ratio: 10-to-1
Carburetion: Single two-barrel
Horsepower: 315 @ 4100 rpm
Torque: 465 lbs-ft @ 2200 rpm
Transmission: Three-speed automatic
Rear Axle Ratio: 2.89

Performance

Gas Mileage: 11 to 14 miles per gallon
Acceleration: 0-30 mph in 4.9 seconds, 0-45 mph in 8.3 seconds and 0-60 mph in 14.2 seconds
Speedometer Error: Indicated 30, 45 and 60 mph are actual 28, 42.5 and 54.5 mph respectively
Power-Weight Ratio: 16.8 lbs. per horsepower
Horsepower Per Cubic Inch: .68

CADILLAC

a decrease in length and option offerings

CADILLAC'S LEADERSHIP in the luxury class of U.S. cars is undisputed. As such it undoubtedly is a kind of bellwether, a fact which makes its 1961 major changes in design direction of particular interest and significance.

The net results of these changes are shorter cars, simplification of engine options and a retrenchment in the special series offerings that in the past have been a conspicuous feature of the Cadillac line.

The mark of a domestic prestige car in general, and with Cadillac in particular, until now has been impressiveness from massive size. For the new model year, however, the Cadillacs are approximately three inches shorter than in 1960. The 1961 Cadillacs, outside the limousine category, are 222 inches long, compared with 225 inches of the preceding models. And even the limousines have been shortened from 245 inches to 242.

None of the car's other exterior dimensions have been significantly altered. Where there are differences from 1960, they amount to no more than fractions of an inch. Widths of the different series and body types average out to close to 80 inches, overall height 56 inches.

The engine picture couldn't be simpler. There is just one Cadillac engine for all series, a 390-cubic-inch V-8 rated at 325 hp. This is the same plant that served most Cadillacs last year, with a four-barrel carburetor. Not available are any higher horsepower options, such as the 1960 345-hp unit that used three two-barrel carburetors. All series, of course, have the Hydramatic automatic as the standard transmission with a 2.94 axle ratio, except the limousines, which use a 3.36 gearing.

There are three series of 1961 Cadillacs: the Fleetwood 60, the 62 and the 75 limousine series. The basic body types are similar to those of preceding model years, with one very notable exception.

Gone are the super-luxury cars that represented the ultimate in prestige. The famed Eldorado series of the 1950's has been reduced to the position of a name only for one version of the 62 series. And dropped entirely is the limited-production Eldorado Brougham that once had a $10,000-plus price tag. The top-of-the-line now is the Fleetwood 60 Special, which in 1961 has special styling characteristics.

It was Cadillac that led the GM parade several years ago into the age of the full-wrap windshield that also resulted in elbow or dogleg front pillar that seriously interfered with easy and graceful front-seat entry and exit. This design defect has now been remedied by adopting a new pillar that slopes, rather than forming a sharp angle, and is the most satisfactory solution.

Cadillac also has devised doors that are wider and swing open further for the 1961 models. New interior feature is a glove box of the bin type.

Engineering innovations include the crankcase ventilation device for California cars; a chassis that is claimed to be completely lubrication-free; and despite the aforementioned unchanged dimensions, except the reduction in body length, the effective turning circle of the car has been trimmed by a full three feet down to 43 feet.

The 1961 Cadillacs, therefore, emerge as more "compact" cars, using the term in an especially broad sense, and certainly more maneuverable. A short step but definitely in a different direction.

/MT

Instrument panel of the 1961 Cadillac is newly designed with emphasis on greater visibility and easier operation. Shown below are the Sedan de Ville and Biarritz convertible of the "Sixty-Two" series.

1961 Cadillac Engineering

In any discussion pertaining to the mechanical and engineering qualities of the 1961 Cadillac, the key words must be *greater comfort*. Much has been done to make operation of the 1961 Cadillac even more pleasant for all occupants.

The 1961 body is more convenient to get in and out . . . head room is increased, as is leg room . . . and seating comfort is increased with greater chair height.

Additionally, important advancements have been made in ride, handling ease, quietness of operation and braking.

Entrance and exit convenience is improved as a result of the forward sloping windshield pillar, by a rear door that opens seven-and-one-half inches further, by moving forward the center stub pillar, by narrowing the rocker step-over, and by increasing door opening heights.

Considerable improvement is made in head room, leg room and seating comfort. Here is how this has been accomplished. The chassis and frame modification permit lowering of the front floor, giving greater chair height for improved seating and greater leg room. Seat cushions are deepened. The tunnel is narrower and lower, resulting from the repositioning of the engine and transmission.

The continuing ride developments come from the new front suspension and structural advances possible with the new body.

Additional improvements in ease of handling result from the increased boost from the new steering pump. So less effort is required in steering or parking. Also, the car is more maneuverable—turning in a 43 foot circle, three feet less than last year.

Still another form of comfort—quietness and smoothness of operation—has advanced even further in 1961. This comes about as a result of the new front suspension and the improved body structure. The new structure permits the reduction of several mounts in the center of the body, eliminating points of noise and vibration transmission from the chassis to the body. A new type rubber support for the propeller shaft bearing adds to quietness and smoothness of the drive line.

As regards braking improvement, greater gains have been made than the substantial progress of last year. And this, too, is related to the new front suspension. The new suspension design permits the moving of front brake drums into the air stream. By adding fins onto the extended drums greater cooling results. This permits use of a larger wheel cylinder with shorter stopping distances and greater freedom from pull and squeak.

Other engineering advancements on the 1961 Cadillac include a lubrication free chassis, a new windshield wiper system covering 15 percent greater wiping area, a single exhaust system for greater life and an anti-smog kit that will be standard on all California bound cars and optional elsewhere.

Another option offered for the first time is a rear window defogger.

In the rear compartment of Cadillac sedans, the rear door swings open an additional 7½ inches and is 6 inches wider. The narrower step-over sill adds inches to the usable width of the floor, thanks to the improved body structure.

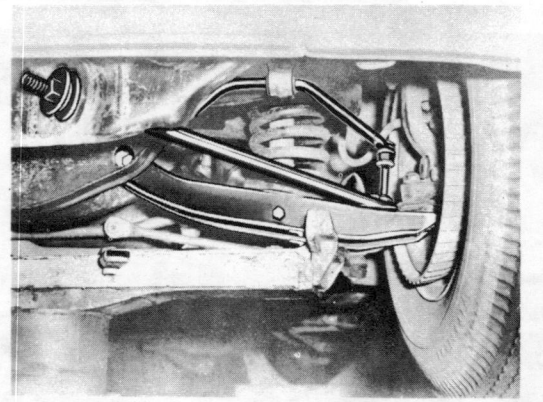

In the all-new Cadillac front suspension, the lower control arm is connected at only two points: one at the steering knuckle, and one at the frame as compared to three points on previous models. To stabilize the front suspension, a diagonal tie strut is used with each lower suspension arm.

Entrance and exit convenience in the 1961 Cadillac is improved as a result of sloping the front windshield pillar, eliminating the dog leg.

MORE THAN ANY OTHER single Detroit car, Cadillac has come to symbolize those things that the luxury class stands for. The road test conclusions indicate that this is largely justified. Strangely, Cadillac also has the most conservative overall design of any car in the luxury field. Undoubtedly the reason for this is that Cadillac long ago won its spurs as a prestige car and no longer needs to use startling gimmicks or garish ornamentation to make the car different.

The test car, a Sedan de Ville, was a four-door hardtop which Cadillac identifies as a six-window model. Essentially all closed Cadillacs are hardtops, the main difference being in the roof style. A four-window style has a flat roof with a bigger rear window. Rounding out the line are two convertibles and the limousines.

Cadillac has only one powerplant this year, the 390-cubic-inch V-8 that has been revised several times since it first appeared in 1949. There have been no basic changes this year except that no options are offered; the triple two-barrel version of last year has been dropped. The four-barrel version of the test car produces 325 hp at 4800 rpm and 430 lbs.-ft. of torque at 3100 rpm.

The rear axle ratio was 3.21-to-1. Three other gearsets are available, 2.94, 3.36 and 3.77. However, Cadillac does not encourage interchanging the ratios and flatly states that the 3.21 is mandatory when equipped with air conditioning.

When the acceleration tests were finished, Cadillac proved to be the best performer of the three, but only by one-tenth of a second at the 0-60-mph mark. Judged by a broader scope of cars, it falls into the moderately better performers. Of course, the luxury class no longer is rated against the hot cars, and Cadillac's performance is normal for its class.

Along with its better performance and higher gearing, the Cadillac turned in what is usually considered normal gasoline economy for its class. The 8-to-12-mpg average, however, is considerably lower than most standard-size sedans.

Cadillac's most obvious quality is a good ride with reasonably good stability at high speeds. Stability is considerably improved over last year, when the car had a tendency to wallow at highway speeds.

The better stability can probably be traced to a redesigned front suspension. Last year the wishbone-type arm was held rigid at three points — steering knuckle

CADILLAC

A NEW TREND TO CONSERVATIVE LUXURY

and two places on the frame. This year Cadillac engineers have connected the lower control arm at one place on the frame and on the steering knuckle. A diagonal tie strut is used to control fore-and-aft deflection of the front wheels.

Besides helping improve the stability and ride, the new suspension design made it possible to move the front brake drums into the air stream. By adding fins onto the extended drums, greater cooling results. Since the wheel cylinders are larger, brakes are more efficient, with less fade.

Each year Cadillac adds some kind of additional sound insulation. This year there is a new rubber support for the intermediate propeller shaft bearing and all the joints in the suspension are made through rubber bushings, which act as road noise isolators. So complete is the insulation, in fact, that engineers had to add a copper strap from the suspension to the frame to keep tire static out of the radio.

All this insulation actually made little difference inside the passenger compartment. In last year's test, no mechanical noises were detected, and this year the same proved true. Inside, only the loudest of outside noises ever came through when the windows were rolled up.

Power steering is standard equipment and has practically no feel of the road. At any speed all driving is done visually, with no road shocks to tell the driver what is happening. There has been a change in the power unit so that even less effort is now required. Another change in the steering geometry (the steering circle is three feet less) makes the car more maneuverable. This has been fairly effective, and getting into and out of tight parking spaces is noticeably easier.

Cadillac has a new body this year, but the styling is so close to last year's that most of the design benefits could easily be overlooked. At the front door the dogleg has been eliminated, greatly improving entry and exit. But a more important change is in the rear door, which is six inches wider and opens 7½ inches farther. This makes getting into and out of the back seat exceptionally good, in fact, probably the easiest of any domestic four-door sedan. This is a major quality in a luxury sedan, where the back seat is often as important as the front.

Cadillac's back seat is one of Detroit's roomiest, with more than generous legroom. In front the dimensions are only average, although ample. The upholstery padding was firmer than any other car in Cadillac's class, although this in no way interfered with comfort. In fact, for most drivers on long trips the firmer padding was preferred. The upholstery material was only average for the luxury class (there are 112 others available, ranging up to the most expensive fabrics), but it was durable, attractive and well fitted.

Along with its conservative interior, Cadillac has a conservative dash panel and

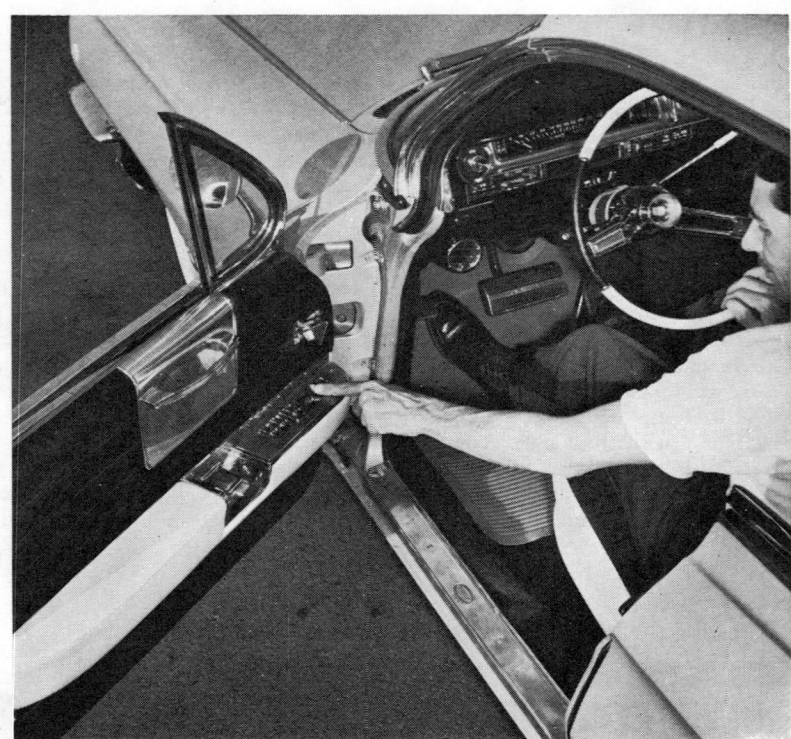

Driver control buttons are arranged in practical and extremely convenient layout. Nearly all controls can be operated with left hand, and many of these without moving arm from the armrest.

driver controls — although there are more controls than are found on the average sedan. However, the layout is extraordinarily practical. Without moving his left arm from the armrest the driver can open the door, lock or unlock all doors, open or close any window or either front vent, adjust the front seat six ways or adjust the outside rear view mirror. Within easy reach of his left hand the driver can also set the Cruise Control to a desired speed and turn on the lights, air conditioning or windshield wiper. On the right are only three controls ordinarily used when driv-

Cadillac's engine compartment is exceptionally crowded. Notice components placed in front of radiator.

ing: radio, heater and ignition. Once the radio is on and the volume adjusted, stations can be changed with a foot control. This means that the right hand is seldom necessary for any adjustments. This is an excellent arrangement; since most people are right-handed, it is only natural to assume that driving would be safer if the left hand is removed from the wheel.

The glove compartment is new this year and has been designed like a bin. This, Cadillac claims, makes it virtually impossible for anything to roll out. But since it is so small, it is practically impossible to get enough in it to worry about the contents spilling out.

Another new interior feature is the steering wheel, which is 16 inches in diameter, one inch smaller than last year. The smaller wheel is possible, no doubt, because of the more effective power steering, but is also a psychological factor in making the interior seem larger.

One accessory, the power deck lid lock, is a switch inside the glove compartment. It works slightly different from other similar devices, in that it unlocks the trunk and only raises the deck lid slightly. Even though the trunk space is rated high in cubic capacity, it is not as efficiently laid out as it could be — and lacks the deep well arangement of many other GM standard-size sedans.

1961 CADILLAC

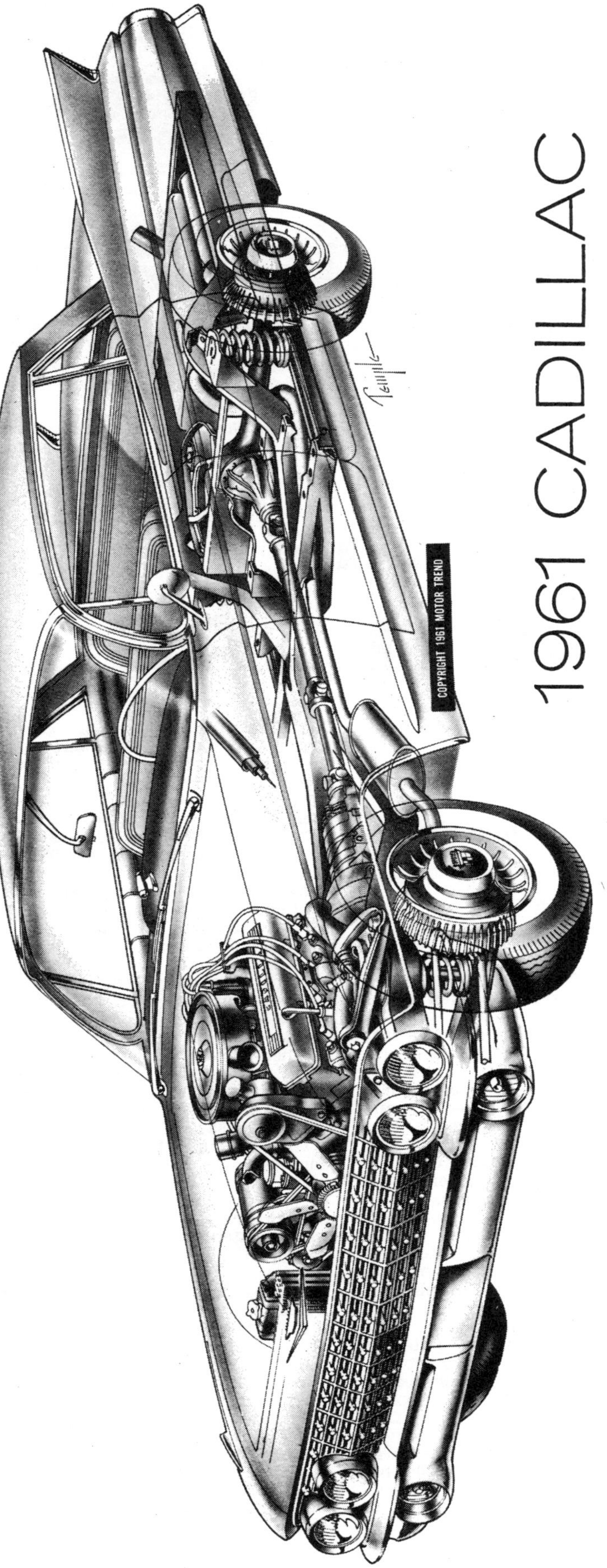

test car
TEST CAR: Cadillac Sedan de Ville
BODY TYPE: 4-door hardtop
BASE PRICE: $5498

maneuverability factors
OVERALL LENGTH: 222 inches
OVERALL WIDTH: 79.8 inches
OVERALL HEIGHT: 56.3 inches
WHEELBASE: 129.5 inches
TREAD, FRONT/REAR: 61 and 61 inches
SHIPPING WEIGHT: 4710 lbs.
STEERING: 3.7 turns lock-to-lock
TURNING CIRCLE: 43 feet curb-to-curb
GROUND CLEARANCE: 5.3 inches

interior room
SEATING CAPACITY: Six
FRONT SEAT
  HEADROOM: 34.3 inches
  HIPROOM: 59.7 inches
  LEGROOM: 45.6 inches
TRUNK CAPACITY: 17 cubic feet

engine & drive train
TYPE: Ohv V-8
DISPLACEMENT: 390 cubic inches
BORE & STROKE: 4.0 x 3.8
COMPRESSION RATIO: 10.25-to-1
CARBURETION: Single 4-barrel
HORSEPOWER: 325 @ 4800 rpm
TORQUE: 430 @ 3100 rpm
TRANSMISSION: Automatic
REAR AXLE RATIO: 3.21

performance
GAS MILEAGE: 8 to 12 miles per gallon
ACCELERATION: 0-30 mph in 3.8 seconds, 0-45 mph in 6.7 seconds and 0-60 mph in 10.4 seconds
SPEEDOMETER ERROR: Indicated 30, 45 and 60 mph are actual 29.5, 44 and 58.5 mph respectively
ODOMETER ERROR: Indicated 100 miles is actual 96.5 miles
WEIGHT-POWER RATIO: 14.5 lbs. per horsepower
HORSEPOWER PER CUBIC INCH: .834

Initial shipment of Caddies is limited to cheaper and smaller Series 62. Imported as left hand drive cars, they are yet to be converted.

Return of the CADILLAC

After many years of absence, Cadillac cars are now being sold again in Australia. Prices range £6000 upwards, depending on the styling you choose.

By PETER HALL

JUST before the Second World War came to upset the normal way of life in Australia there were few cars made anywhere in the world that could not be bought off the showroom floor by those who had the cash or were a reasonable credit risk.

Among the more popular of the fancy cars, in circles where there was enough lucre to justify more than just an idle thought about such matters, was the American-built, and always fully-imported, Cadillac.

Melbourne and Sydney Cadillac admirers, in particular, were well catered for by Rhodes and Lober's, respectively. Of course, many other General Motors dealers — especially in wealthy country areas — had the franchise to sell Cadillacs and their close but unfortunately late relation, La Salle.

In a land where Rolls-Royce was and is, clearly the greatest symbol of worldly success, the Cadillac never achieved quite the status in eyes of the general populus as it did in its home country and among the Arabs.

But it did well and Rhodes, Lobers and numerous other GM dealers were dissatisfied with the fact of war for other reasons as well as the patriotic ones.

They had high hopes when the war ended that things would return at least to pre-war normal.

But things were not to be so rosy. A tremendous world-wide demand for new cars and a simultaneous shortage of them limited severely the numbers of cars that could be brought into Australia, either in bits or wholly made up overseas.

As far as Cadillac was concerned, few were made in the first year or two after hostilities ceased and those that did come off the production line were quickly gobbled by the hungry American market.

Then, when production increased and it may have been possible to order a few dozen for Australia, government policy here resulted in almost a total ban on the importation of luxury American cars. Dollars were very, very scarce.

A few Cadillacs did find their way to our shores during the 1950s, but most of them were bought by Australians who had dollar funds of their own in America or by American nationals who were working in Australia for a time and brought the cars with them. They were often eventually sold here. A few were sneaked in under the Custom's Department's nose, but the department was not slow in seizing them.

So, at least in the Cadillac Fan Club, the first big news of 1961 was that Cadillac cars were back in the showrooms of Australia and were available to sale without any risks of Her Majesty's Customs taking an unwelcome interest in them after they were bought.

More accurately, the cars were available in two Australian showrooms — Rhodes in Melbourne and Lobers in Sydney, who had languished through 20 years of non-Cadillac existence brightened somewhat, in both cases, by possession of Holden franchises. Blow-softeners, as you might say.

The buyers who came to the showrooms to inspect the first shipment did not actually stampede. Inquiry was reported to be good and a surprisingly large number of orders were written considering the period of crippling sales tax and credit restriction.

Rhodes were so confident they would do well with Cadillac after the 20-year famine that they imported half a dozen in the initial for stock on spec.

Most of the Cadillacs which had arrived at the time of writing were from the relatively small Series 62 range.

Long (18½ feet), lavish and very glamorous in the American style, they retail at slightly under £6000 including the new 40 percent sales tax.

RETURN OF THE CADILLAC

The price is almost a pleasant surprise for many potential Cadillac owners who thought more in terms of £7000 or £8000. They forgot (or never knew) that Cadillac prices in the United States range from as low as the medium price bracket (about 4000 dollars) right up to 13,000 dollars plus for extraordinarily lavish Eldorado Brougham which, among other things, has an unpainted stainless steel roof.

An absolute retail price has not yet been fixed for the Cadillac in Australia, because neither Rhodes nor Lobers have yet converted any of the cars from left to right drive. They have decided to do their own conversions and are joining forces to the extent of swapping expert personnel and exchanging know-how. A Rhodes executive told me they were allowing a generous sum for the conversion and would pass on the almost inevitable savings when the actual cost was finalised, to the customer.

Final price of the car should be between £5850 and £6000.

For that money the Cadillac buyer will get a powerful, luxurious motor car with almost every aid to lazyman's driving that America has yet invented.

He will get a massive 390 cubic inch overhead valve V8 engine that develops something over 300 bhp on the SAE figure. (The American engine had a compression ratio of 10.5 to 1 and develops 325 bhp at 4800 rpm. The models exported to Australia have been fitted with 8.75 to 1 export engines and develop an unknown amount of horsepower on that ratio.)

He will get power steering, a four-speed Hydramatic automatic transmission that is probably the best automatic available in the world today, power-operated windows and front seat and a magnificent fully-automatic American radio.

Other sumptuous features of the car include four cigarette lighters, thick black carpet and black and grey synthetic upholstery.

During a brief drive of a brand new Cadillac that had had no service other than a wash since it left the ship, I found it was everything a Caddy is expected to be — easy to drive, a crowd puller and very comfortable indeed.

\#

Much desired by Australians in the years since the war, the Cadillac is now back on the market. Prices are high, ranging upwards from £6000.

In the popular hardtop sedan body style, this Caddie is 18½ feet long, has huge V8 engine of 390 cu in capacity. Transmission is four speed.

THREE

for the MONEY

AMERICA'S LEADING LUXURY CARS — CADILLAC, IMPERIAL AND THE LINCOLN CONTINENTAL — REFLECT SUMPTUOUS STYLE AND TASTE.

Luxury personified: Cadillac, Imperial, Lincoln...
"A look, a feel, a state of mind"

by Bob Russo

THE LEADING LUXURY CARS in America today — Cadillac, Imperial and Lincoln — share one significant point. Each has dignity, that unmistakable characteristic which sets a thoroughbred apart from the cow pony. This quality may be expressed and reflected differently by each manufacturer but it has a common appeal in "look, feel and state of mind" for those who drive these cars — or those who wish they could drive them.

In this test of the Cadillac de Ville, Imperial LeBaron and Lincoln Continental, our purpose is not to evaluate them by comparison but to pick out the major points of each model on which the greatest emphasis has been placed.

The 1961 Cadillac de Ville, in keeping with the entire Cadillac line, emphasizes *greater* comfort. This has been achieved through a change in chassis and frame construction which permits more head- and legroom, and an improved ride through a new front suspension system. Body style has taken on only a slight change, noticeable mostly in the rear where tail/back-up light pods are now in a horizontal position rather than vertical. Power steering and brakes and Hydra-Matic transmissions are, of course, standard on all 1961 Cadillacs.

steel appliques at the roof insert area and a "town car" rear window which offers greater privacy to passengers.

The instrument panel is one of the most functional in any car, regardless of price. The entire interior, in fact, shows good taste and careful planning. There is no cramping for leg space, even for rear seat passengers, when the front seat is in its rearmost position.

Considerable styling changes this year give the LeBaron a classic look. Tail fins have been subdued, but the trunk lid with the familiar wheel cover is still available as an option. Emphasis has shifted more to the front of the car, where crisp lines are met by a distinguished grille and free-standing headlights.

Driving the LeBaron provides every bit of the big car feel one would expect from a luxury vehicle such as this. But despite this big car feel, the Imperial handles exceptionally well. Our one objection was vision, side and rear. Not being able to see the right front fender takes a bit of getting used to, while the vision restriction created by the town-car rear window requires extreme caution when leaving a parking place or moving into a busy street from a side road.

The Continental, available as a sedan or convertible and

If a comparison were to be made, the de Ville has a more racy appearance with its sweeping fins, large windows and peppy performance — in contrast with a slight trace of European styling found in the Imperial and Lincoln.

The luxury of a smooth, quiet ride for which Cadillac has always been famous, has been further improved with a redesigned frame and chassis, permitting use of a new suspension system, front and rear. Road bumps are better absorbed through the new single lower control arm in front, while noise is dampened with generous use of rubber mountings throughout the frame and chassis.

The same 390-cubic-inch V-8 engine with its 325-hp rating has been retained for '61. It packs a surprising amount of wallop despite the weight of the car, and will make the 0-60 run in 11 seconds.

Vision, from all angles, is excellent from the driver's seat, and the de Ville is a true comfort to drive. Despite its size, it moves through traffic easily, has plenty of reserve power if needed for passing, and will brake to a halt from 60 mph in 175 feet.

The Imperial LeBaron, most elegant of the four Imperial models available this year, contains just about every luxury ever invented for an automobile, and most of these are standard equipment, including power seats, windows, brakes and steering, automatic transmission, and windshield washers. One of its most striking points, perhaps, is the smooth body finish. Almost flawless, it complements the fine styling of the LeBaron which is emphasized by sculptured stainless

the only Lincoln model now made, has been designed to fit its name. Inside and out, it has the continental touch. Massive bumpers, slender roof and unbroken body lines give it a distinctive look that is all Lincoln. Seating, especially from a driver's standpoint, is more comfortable than the most expensive easy chair, with a small, thin-rimmed steering wheel well positioned for maximum comfort.

Although not lacking in power, the 430-cubic-inch V-8 engine could use a bit more top-end punch, especially for passing. Its 0-60-mph rating is 13.5 seconds, as compared to 11.0 and 11.1 seconds respectively for Cadillac and Imperial.

Pointing out the Continental's reliability, Henry Ford II revealed at announcement time that the warranty on all 1961 models has been increased to two full years or 24,000 miles — double that offered by other U.S. manufacturers, and an expression of confidence that this is the finest, most reliable luxury car ever produced by the Ford Motor Co.

As mentioned at the beginning, this test of the three leading luxury cars is not meant to compare one against the other. However, one factor that should be pointed out is fuel economy. As expected, none of these cars is easy on gas. The Cadillac averaged nine to 10 mpg, as compared to eight to 10 by the Lincoln and 10 to 12 mpg by the Imperial.

However, fuel economy is not the main reason owners purchase a Cadillac, Lincoln or Imperial. There is a *luxury feeling* that comes with riding in a luxury car that cannot be defined — but it can be bought.

Cadillac Coupe de Ville

Cadillac wheel cover, enhanced by its familiar emblem, gives appearance of cast aluminum. The wheels are steel.

Mounted in rubber at three points, 390-cubic-inch engine is unchanged from '60 models. It has 10.5:1 compression and a four-barrel carburetor to boost horsepower to 325. Pistons are aluminum alloy, slipper-type to help minimize friction.

New, overall power steering has a ratio of 18.2 to 1. Turning angle has been increased from 36 degrees to 38.5, giving quicker, easier response.

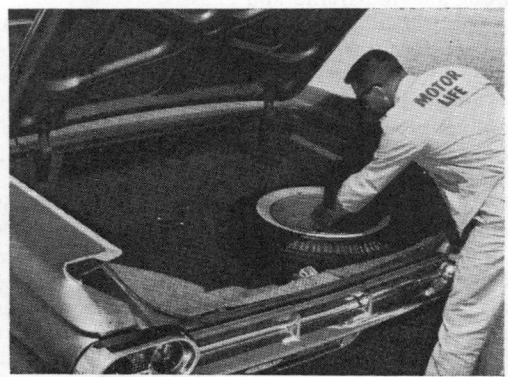

Entire truck floor is carpeted and sealed tight to keep out dust, protect luggage. Flat-mounted spare is fitted with cover for added protection.

CADILLAC
Coupe de Ville

OPTIONS ON CAR TESTED: Power seats and windows, air conditioning, radio, heater, Guide-Matic headlight control

ODOMETER READING AT START OF TEST: 4322 miles

PERFORMANCE

ACCELERATION (2 aboard)
- 0-30 mph............................. 4.0 secs.
- 0-45 mph............................. 7.2
- 0-60 mph............................. 11.0

Standing start ¼-mile 19.0 secs. and 78 mph

Speeds in gears @ 4200 rpm
- 1st .... 22 mph
- 2nd .... 38 mph
- 3rd .... 70 mph

Speedometer Error on Test Car
Car's speedometer reading	31	47	54	64	75	85
Weston electric speedometer	30	45	50	60	70	80

Miles per hour per 1000 rpm in top gear (actual meter reading)...22.5 mph

Stopping Distances — from 30 mph, 33 ft.; from 60 mph, 175 ft.

SPECIFICATIONS FROM MANUFACTURER

Engine
Ohv V-8
Bore: 4.0 ins.   Stroke: 3.875 ins.
Displacement: 390 cubic inches
Compression ratio: 10.5:1
Horsepower: 325 @ 4800 rpm
Ignition: 12-volt battery/coil

Gearbox
Hydra-Matic

Driveshaft
Open

Differential
Hypoid ring & pinion gears
Standard ratio 2.94:1

Suspension
Front: Spherical joint with Cadillac helical-coil springs, direct-acting shocks

Rear: Four-link drive with helical-coil springs, direct-acting shocks

Wheels and Tires
Slotted steel disc wheels with 4-ply, 8.00 x 15 tubeless tires

Brakes
Power brakes standard, with self-adjusting shoes and finned drums
Front and rear: 12-in. drums

Body and Frame
Tubular center "X" frame
Wheelbase 129.5 ins.
Track, front 61 ins., rear 61 ins.
Overall length 222 ins.

Cad's instrument panel includes power antenna and headlight control unit for dimming lights automatically. Modest use of chrome keeps glare and annoying reflections at minimum.

(Right) Power seat and window controls are within easy reach of the driver. Redesigned windshield pillars and higher door openings allow easier entrance and exit.

Most noticeable difference in 1961 Cadillac over 1960 model are horizontally positioned tail lights. Bottom fin, which extends from bumper end to front fender, is also new for '61.

The 1962 Cadillac Fleetwood Sixty Special retains its distinctive upper structure not shared by any other motorcar. The rear of the car presents a new deck lid with a beveled edge and a new cove molding that features a pattern similar to the front grille.

60th Anniversary Cadillacs

Beginning its sixtieth year in the automobile industry, Cadillac is now presenting for 1962 the most complete and competitive line of new models in the Division's history, according to Harold G. Warner, Cadillac general manager and vice president of General Motors.

"A dramatically new silhouette, outstanding engineering achievements and important safety features, new to any American motorcar, are combined in our anniversary automobile," Warner said.

"As the records show, safety always is of prime concern to Cadillac each year. This year is no exception. In fact, in 1962 there is even more emphasis on safety with a new dual braking system and significant lighting developments, both in the front and rear of the automobile," Warner points out.

In this anniversary year, Cadillac is offering 12 models, the same as last year. Five of the 12 will feature a classic new roof design giving an entirely new silhouette to the car and changing the over-all styling personality.

This sleek and low roof design which reflects the leadership of last year's Fleetwood Sixty Special Sedan appears on the Four-Window Sedan de Ville, the Coupe de Ville, Sixty-Two Coupe, Town Sedan and Park Avenue Sedan.

Wheelbase is unchanged: 129.5 inches on all models except the Series Seventy-Five Sedan and Limousine at 149.8 inches. Overall length remains at 222 inches on eight models, while the Series Seventy-Five Sedan and Limousine again are 242.3 inches in length. The new Park Avenue Sedan joins the Town Sedan at 215 inches. Overall width also is unchanged.

The two 215 inch sedan models have the exact interior dimensions as the new Four-Window de Ville. The seven inch difference in length comes out fo the rear deck and trunk. These two models will differ in interior trim and appointments. The Town Sedan has the Sixty-Two interior selections while the Park Avenue uses the de Ville interiors.

To create a more massive appearance, all 12 models have a new grille with the traditional Cadillac cross-hatch design which in profile is more vertical. Contributing to the broad shouldered look, the grille design also forms a background for the headlamps. A new Cadillac script appears on the grille.

The rear quarter styling is an excellent reflection of the 1962 design character. The fins are low and sleek. The new bumper end and taillight housing provides a solid visual anchor for the strong horizontal design lines of the body, and the use of chrome is held to a minimum.

The rear appearance of the car is enhanced by a new deck lid with a beveled edge in keeping with the crisp and angular styling motif of 1962.

Between the deck lid and rear bumper is a new ribbed cove molding of extruded aluminum which is painted the body color. On the Fleetwood Sixty Special and the Eldorado Biarritz this molding resembles the front grille.

Styling and engineering combine to bring exciting new lighting developments to the industry. At the side of the headlamps as an integral part of the front end appearance is a new cornering light, which illuminates the way into a turn at night. The taillight in the rear bumper also is completely new and houses a taillamp, stop lamp, turn signal light and back-up light. Yet under normal daytime operations the exterior lens appears white.

The dignified Sixty Special retains its distinctive upper structure not shared by any other motorcar.

The Eldorado Biarritz Convertible has a new body side molding which is painted to match the interior and bordered in chrome with Eldorado identification at the forward end.

The new deeply-drawn wheel disc is a finely tailored combination of chrome and matching body color.

There are 16 standard exterior colors available—one more than in 1961—plus five special Eldorado colors.

With tailoring and selection the finest ever offered, the exterior styling beauty of the 1962 Cadillac is fully complemented with new elegant and refined interiors. Wool broadcloths, natural grain leathers and the latest contemporary fabrics are featured in newly styled interiors.

A total of 92 interior options are available. Among the new highlights of interior styling are the inclusion of wool broadcloth trim for Series Sixty-Two models, handsome fabric options in the Biarritz Convertible and a greatly expanded selection of leathers and bucket seats in the de Ville models.

Interior elegance achieves new heights in the Fleetwood Sixty Special. The interior appointments of this motorcar are highlighted by large cherry veneer panels in all doors, an embroidered crest and laurel leaf design on the front and rear center arm rests and new reading lights on the upper rear quarter panels.

Unquestionably the major contribution to safer driving is the new three-way brake system on the 1962 Cadillac, the first of its kind in the automobile industry. Heart of the system is a dual-type power brake master cylinder with a separate piston and brake fluid reservoir for front and rear brakes. From a safety standpoint, this system is ideal because if one of the hydraulic lines is severed, only one pair of wheel brakes would be out of commission.

With the parking brake, which again this year can be employed as a true auxiliary brake, the 1962 Cadillac has three separate brake systems in an emergency. Faster braking also is achieved through a new suspended vacuum booster.

Another engineering first for the industry is a new cornering light which is introduced on all the 1962 Cadillacs. The steady beam angles out from the side of the headlamp, lighting the driver's way into a turn. It is activated by the turn signal lever when the headlights, parking lights, or fog lamps are on.

Also a Cadillac first is the unique new taillight, stoplight and turn signal—yet, it has a white lens in normal daylight operation. The lens shows white when backing up, but shines red when the taillight, stoplight, or turn signal are in operation.

Another safety innovation appearing on all 1962 Cadillacs is a vinyl-backed rear view mirror and vanity mirror, providing shatter proof construction in case of an accident. And seat belt anchors are provided as standard.

Changes in the front spring rate, new front and rear suspension bushings and re-valving of the shock absorbers give a silky smooth ride. Frame modifications and new bearings which reduce friction in the steering linkage provide sureness in ride and handling.

To give additional quietness, a new sound deadening material is used under the floor pan and in the cowl section between the front doors and front fenders. The roof is completely lined with a new sound deadening material for further noise isolation.

Significant chassis refinements include specially cut gears in the transmission, drive line improvements and new exhaust line mountings, all contributing to the quietness of operation.

New in 1962 is a 26-gallon gas tank which will be standard on all models except the Town Sedan and Park Avenue Sedan de Ville. They retain the 21-gallon tank.

The reliable 390 cubic inch V-8 engine remains unchanged in specifications with 325 horsepower and a 10.5 to 1 compression ratio. However, it is quieter in operation and has still better durability through selective fitting of all main bearings to develop closer fits.

For the first time, the heater will be standard equipment on all 1962 Cadillacs. Air conditioned cars will be quieter due to the use of a newly designed fan clutch and a smaller, lighter yet higher output six-cylinder Freon compressor.

Cadillac offers in 1962 a controlled differential while a new development in lubrication gives added life to the wheel bearings.

Other accessory changes in the new models include a cruise control that has been simplified for driver convenience. It is lighted and is of the wheel type, providing more accurate control.

The automatic trunk lock is now mechanical, rather than electric. The remotely controlled trunk release is now vacuum operated. ★

HANDLING is amazingly good for such a big car: only 3½ turns lock-to-lock, and she's very stable on corners.

EGAD—A CAD!

1961 Cadillac swamps you with comfort and gadgetry, yet performs like an outsize sports car, reports David McKay

A CADILLAC "de Ville" pillarless sedan—favorite of film stars, business tycoons, U.S. trade-union bosses and Middle East oil sheiks—found its way into my unaccustomed hands the other week.

I admit I was somewhat awed at first by the size of the car (18½ feet long, over 6½ feet wide) and the responsibility (a rare, privately owned car "on test" is very different to a run-of-the-mill company demonstrator).

The Caddy was handed over to me by one of its chauffeurs, who gave me a run-down on the masses of knobs, switches and levers.

It was a Friday afternoon, and the thought of suddenly being turned loose in this £6000 "land liner" on the wrong side of town, and having to negotiate the city and the Harbor

ENGINE bay is poorly finished, in contrast to rest of car — and the 6½-litre V8 is almost invisible under its burden of ancillary units.

Bridge before reaching a safe anchorage at home, was almost too much.

But the garage staff, who had gone to the trouble of filling the huge tank with 100-octane fuel and checking over the engine, stood by expectantly, waiting for me to blast off.

I couldn't let them down; so, with great trepidation—disguised, I hoped, with great nonchalance—I edged into the traffic stream and away.

As soon as I became accustomed to the incredibly direct steering (3½ turns lock-to-lock), made even more surprising with power assistance, and the excellent manoeuvrability for such a vast car, I relaxed and enjoyed it.

I began to look around and at once felt like a fish in a bowl. It was knock-off time in the city, and I could have filled the Caddy a dozen times over, judging from the welcoming smiles we got from admiring passers-by.

But I had work to do—the Caddy was for testing. I pulled alongside a Bentley and was amazed to see how low the Caddy was in comparison. The other car towered above us like a double-decker—a quality double-decker, of course.

Cook's Tour

Safely home, I got my first chance to inspect the car without interruptions.

Apart from its tailfins — so sharp that I was afraid a bumptious Morris Minor was going to impale itself on them at one stage — the Cadillac has good, clean lines, enhanced by its pillarless construction, and is free of the garish chromework once favored by its makers.

I lifted the bonnet ("hood" to a Caddy driver) — without, I might add, needing to release any catch inside the car. You'd have thought General Motors would provide an internal bonnet lock on their most expensive product!

What I saw underneath didn't tally with my expectations, either. The engine, for all its 325 horses, looked like any other big American V8, decidedly lacking in finish. The only difference was in the larger-than-usual number of ancillaries crowded into the compartment.

At the same time, however, it impressed one as the sort of engine that would stand up to the abuse of some illiterate sheik, such as I had met driving earlier Cadillac models in Irak, back in 1955.

The array of ancillaries is really something. In addition to the normal equipment, it includes units to operate power steering and power brakes — plus a miniature powerhouse to supply energy for the electrically-controlled doorlocks, windows, seats, warming and refrigerating plants, radio aerial, and so on.

PILLARLESS look goes well with long, low body.

MAIN SPECIFICATIONS

ENGINE: V8, o.h.v.; bore 101.6mm., stroke 98.4mm., capacity 6392c.c.; compression ratio 10.5 to 1; maximum b.h.p. 325 at 4800 r.p.m.; maximum torque 430ft./lb. at 3100 r.p.m.; single 4-choke downdraught Carter carburettor, mechanical fuel pump; 12v. ignition.

TRANSMISSION: G.M. Hydra-Matic 4-speed, with special lever position to restrict drive to the three lower ratios; overall ratios—1st, 11.6; 2nd, 7.5; 3rd, 4.5; top, 2.9 to 1.

SUSPENSION: Front independent, by coil springs and tie-struts; coil springs at rear; telescopic hydraulic shock-absorbers all round.

STEERING: Recirculating-ball type, power-operated; 3½ turns lock-to-lock, 45ft. turning circle.

WHEELS: Pressed-steel discs, with 8.00 by 15in. tyres.

CONSTRUCTION: Separate tubular centre X-frame.

DIMENSIONS: Wheelbase 10ft. 9½in.; track, 5ft. 1in. front and rear; length 18ft. 6in., width 6ft. 7in., height 4ft. 8in.; ground clearance 5in.

KERB WEIGHT: 45cwt.

FUEL TANK: 17½ gallons.

PERFORMANCE ON TEST

CONDITIONS: Fine, cool, no wind; dry bitumen; two occupants, 100-octane fuel.

BEST SPEED: 110 m.p.h.

STANDING quarter-mile: 18.6s.

MAXIMUM in indirect ratios: 1st, 30 m.p.h.; 2nd, 60; 3rd, 85.

ACCELERATION from rest through gears; 0-30, 3.0s.; 0-40, 5.0s.; 0-50, 7.4s.; 0-60, 11.0s.; 0-70, 14.6s.; 0-80, 19.0s.

HILLCLIMB: 2min. 33s.

MOUNTAIN CIRCUIT: 50 m.p.h. average.

BRAKING: 31ft. to stop from 30 m.p.h. in neutral.

FUEL CONSUMPTION: 12.2 m.p.g. overall.

PRICE: On application (approx. £6000 with tax)

SHARP in more ways than one — that lower fin threatens shins of unwary pedestrians. BELOW: Driver's armrest contains controls to work all windows and doorlocks.

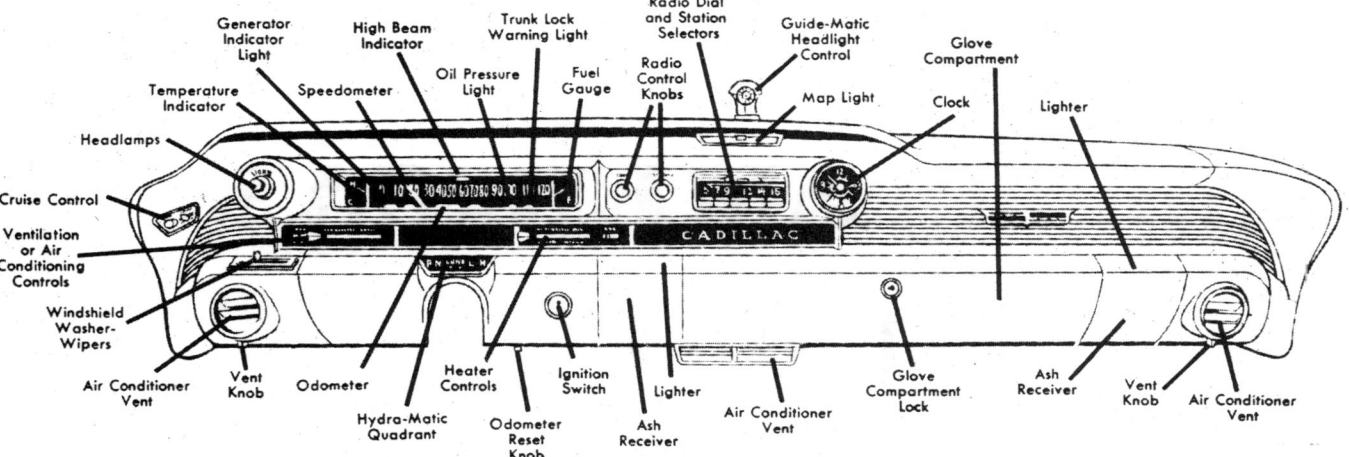

Together with the automatic transmission, all this would probably absorb at least 100 of the engine's horses.

Closing the bonnet, I made an excursion to the back of the car and lifted the boot lid. The cavern under it looked roomy enough to carry a Goggo Dart as a tender.

The big spare wheel, carried flat on the floor, had no cover to protect luggage; but there was a tag on the boot lid, telling you what to do if you got a flat tyre—other than call your nearest Caddy dealer.

The Inside Story

I closed the boot and went and sat inside the car. This, after all, is what a Caddy owner sees most of—and I'll go on record as saying I've never been in a better interior.

Seats are vast, with ample space for six big occupants—and leg-room in the rear compartment is quite exceptional for these days. There are individual armrests, and cigar lighters and ashtrays within easy reach of everyone (a lighter and a tray are built into each rear door).

Upholstery is of fine silk fabric, leather-faced. Leather and polished stainless steel take the place of the wood trim used in "quality" English cars; it's like the difference between a lush apartment in Manhattan and a London club.

Windows go up or down at the touch of an electric switch built into each door, the pushbutton radio (standard equipment) plays with perfect tone and has an electrically operated telescopic aerial.

In contrast to some earlier Caddies, the dash treatment isn't overdone—the Cadillac lettering is neat and restrained, the rather small steering wheel beautifully made.

But the instrumentation is positively primitive. All you get is a speedo, plus gauges for water temperature and fuel—warning lights cover the rest, as they do on the cheapest English or Continental cars.

That's the only fault, though: rest of the equipment couldn't be more generous or efficient.

(Continued on page 73)

LUSH leather padding, stainless steel, deeply-dished steering wheel and a mass of controls (see sketch above). But instruments are few, and accelerator uncomfortably close to parking footbrake. BELOW: Boot is huge—so is the spare wheel, which surely should have a cover to protect luggage.

AMERICA'S LUXURY CARS

MT Road Test
by Wayne Thoms

Cadillac
Imperial
Lincoln Continental

THERE ARE THREE traditionally acknowledged luxury cars that bear Made-in-U.S. tags — Cadillac, Chrysler Imperial and Lincoln Continental. In marked contrast to the trio of imports tested last month, each of which had an individual approach to the luxury concept, our three are more notable for their similarities than their differences. True, each domestic has its own styling and size theme but appointments, gadgets, power assists, and even performance are remarkably the same.

Some of the luxury features are standard, some are tabbed as extra, yet most of these cars normally will carry a maximum load of extras so that they are fitted out almost identically. For example, all include or have available power windows and vent panes, six-way power seats, pull-down center armrest for the front seat, power door locks, electric antenna, remote-control outside mirror, a form of automatic speed-holding, and the expected features, such as air conditioning, power steering and brakes, and automatic transmission.

Since many of these features are available on less expensive models, what, besides high price, makes a luxury car? Obviously, not accessories, and it is certainly not engineering because these cars embody neither radical concepts nor techniques. It can be summed up in one word — quality. This takes in quality of coachwork, which means more care at time of assembly; quality of materials, particularly for interiors where the cars must convey an instant and strong impression of rich, good taste; and quality of mechanical components, as seen in more rigid inspections which will reject mechanisms not up to the highest possible standards. For these reasons one pays substantially more for a luxury car than for more conventional transportation.

There is something else that is essential in the making of a luxury car — state of mind. The cars are recognized as expensive, ergo their possessors are recognized as commanding a certain type of wealth. Such recognition can be important to the ego, or it can be the cold business proposition of putting up a good front. In these cases it is unimportant whether owners recognize and appreciate quality. They buy the name, relying upon the manufacturer's integrity to also furnish them satisfactory transportation. This is the reason, and the primary reason, why a car maker associated with low-cost autos finds it impossible to upgrade his moderately-priced car into the luxury field; conversely, this is why luxury car makers who have tried to downgrade their product in the hope of mass sales have invariably failed in the attempt.

Moving away from the philosophy of luxury, it is pertinent to note the quantity of production relationship among the three makes. Cadillac leads the field, partly because of a wider diversity of models (13) at several price levels, although none of them are low enough to be in the popular price brackets. For the 11 months of 1961, Cad made 128,687 cars, Lincoln produced 27,644 Continentals, and Chrysler built 10,138 Imperials. Whether this ratio is shifting for '62 it is difficult to say. We do know that Imperial is moving into a strong campaign to sell the nation's leading business and professional people. Lincoln has been selling slightly less than half its production to leasing agencies, enabling persons who might otherwise not be able to afford them, to drive Continentals as their own on long-term leases. And there seems to be no shortage of customers for Cadillac dealers.

We learned one thing above all while testing these automobiles: driving America's three finest cars was extremely pleasurable — so enjoyable, in fact, that it was impossible to pick any one car and say categorically that it was the best.

PHOTOS BY PAT BROLLIER

CADILLAC

NOW IN THEIR 60TH YEAR of auto production, Cadillac rolls along in '62 with an enticing selection of 13 models that rank as the largest one-make group of desirable luxury cars in the world. For our test we selected Cad's finest, the Fleetwood Series 60 Special sedan. There is one larger, the Series 75, but it is essentially a limousine on a 149.8-inch wheelbase and we did not feel it truly representative of what most potential Cadillac buyers are seeking.

Because of the close mechanical identity throughout the line, a test of the Fleetwood automatically becomes a test of any '62 Cad. All Cadillacs this year have the same engine, the 325-hp V-8 unchanged from 1961. Except for the big 75, they are all built on a common wheelbase and are 79.9 inches wide. Even length is quite constant at 222 inches. The only exceptions are some shorties in the Series 62 line, which have seven inches cut from the trunk.

The company doesn't exactly give the customer a great choice in power trains. As we said, engines are identical. Hydra-Matic is standard, and all cars carry a 2.94 axle, except when air conditioning is installed, then the ratio becomes 3.21-to-1. Also standard is the heater, power steering, power brakes and electric windows. From this point the sky is the limit in accessory options and interior combinations.

Our test car was equipped with a full load of extras, all of which we found desirable. Their only disadvantage was to increase the price from a suggested retail of $6366 to $7733.63. (This includes $214.43 freight, but not tax and license.)

We felt one thing very strongly about the Cad after a few minutes' exposure — that this is a car which has undergone refinement after refinement over a lengthy period until every detail has a purpose. It was evident in the carefully thought-out driver controls, the near-perfect interior trim and the way in which body panels are assembled to close tolerances. Much of this may be traced to the fact that Cadillac gears its production on a steady year-round basis. Therefore, their craftsmen, who remain year after year, take pride in the car and work accordingly. It helped make us confident that the car would do virtually anything we asked of it, unhesitatingly and well.

Our confidence was well founded in most areas. The car moved out much quicker than most drivers ever will demand. Extremely high speeds can be held for hours on end while the engine loafs along, apparently with little effort. We rated general roadability as only fair because of the high-assist power steering. Wheel pressure is so light that we could almost wish the car around a turn, and there is virtually no road feel. At low speeds where one drives visually this is fine, but at higher velocities most drivers want to be able to sense the road conditions and car attitude through the steering. This would seem to be the price paid for effectively damping noise and shocks from the passenger compartment.

During one stretch of road we were able to experience at first hand the car's tracking ability. Gusty cross-winds became so vicious that trucks and house trailers were stopped by police; yet we drove through and found no problem in correcting our course to compensate for the gusts we later learned were in excess of 60 mph.

One area in which we felt highly confident concerned Cadillac's brakes. Not only do they stop well, they incorporate a dual hydraulic system which will always insure braking on at least two wheels, should a hydraulic line be cut. Only one other American make has this feature — Rambler. Also, the toe-operated parking brake can function as a true emergency brake, usable while the car is moving. We especially liked its operation. There is no release mechanism to forget. It can only be set while the transmission is in NEUTRAL or PARK, and as soon as a gear is engaged the brake releases automatically through vacuum pressure.

We found the ride to be soft and pleasing. Cadillac has combined medium-firm seats with their ride, adding up to a most

Big finned brakes offer effective and insured stopping power. New dual hydraulic system offers braking on at least two wheels even if one unit should go out.

There's room to stretch out and enjoy the elegance of the Fleetwood's interior. On driver's armrest there are controls for windows, locks and mirror.

satisfactory result that invites long hours at the wheel without the weariness often associated with cross-country travel. If silence is golden, then riding in a Cadillac is a 24-karat experience. When the windows were closed and the first-rate vent-heat-cool system turned on, there was no appreciable wind, road or traffic noise to distract passengers.

Eliminating noise takes patient research, and Cadillac's engineers keep dreaming up new ways to quiet the car. This year they have added dense rubber under the floor pan and in the cowl section between the front doors and front fenders to provide additional quieting. Also, they claim specially cut transmission gears, drive line improvements and new exhaust line mounting to keep down the noise. We can testify that it all worked to perfection.

There is a system of accessory controls for the left hand that pleased everyone who drove the car. Without removing the hand from the armrest it was possible to lock or unlock the doors, control all four windows and vent panes, adjust the outside mirror and move the front seat. Setting the Cruise Control is also a left-hand operation. It is wheel-type, mounted above and to the left of the dash.

Cad has two lighting innovations, different from what anyone else offers. At the side of the headlights is a cornering light which throws a 40-degree-wide steady beam whenever the lights are on and the turn signal set. The taillight in the bumper appears white in daylight, yet via a colored filter system it houses taillight, stop light, turn signal and back-up light.

We don't see how anyone can offer any complaints about interior space; our test crew did not. Rear legroom, measured in a bent line from the toeboard to the theoretical base of the spine, is 44.5 inches; comparable figure for the front is 45.6. There is more than ample hiproom (63 inches), with almost enough headroom to wear a hat. Trunk space is typically big Detroit; just toss in the golf bags, suitcases and packages without worry of arranging.

The interior of our Fleetwood had the luxury theme spelled out quietly, but in such a manner that there was no mistaking it. Doors feature handsome wood panels, which one source at Cadillac calls cherry veneer, another terms African Makori wood. Whatever it is, it blends well with the tuft-pleated cloth seats trimmed in soft, gray leather. In addition to the usual dash courtesy lights there are two lights, which Cadillac calls reading lights, on the upper rear quarter panels. Smokers have two big ash trays up front, each with a lighter, plus two more in the rear, also equipped with lighters.

Concerning fuel economy, Cad scored as well as can be expected, considering size and weight. We recorded as much as 13.5 mpg, dropping to nine under adverse conditions. It is liable to fluctuate on either side of those figures, depending upon how the car is driven.

There were a great many things we liked about our Fleetwood, many more than the few we picked upon to illustrate. As with all cars, there were some things we didn't like, but it is such an outstanding motorcar that finding the weak points becomes a tedious search. /MT

CADILLAC FLEETWOOD 60 SPECIAL
4-door, 6-passenger sedan

OPTIONS ON CAR TESTED: Air conditioning, 6-way power seat, whitewall tires, radio with electric antenna, Cruise Control, tinted glass, fog lamps, automatic beam changers, remote trunk lock, power door locks

BASIC PRICE: $6366
PRICE AS TESTED: $7733.63 (plus tax and license)
ODOMETER READING AT START OF TEST: 3456 miles

PERFORMANCE

ACCELERATION (2 aboard)
- 0-30 mph .... 3.7 secs.
- 0-45 mph 6.1
- 0-60 mph 10.8

Standing start ¼-mile 18.9 secs. and 78 mph

Speeds in gears @ shift points
- 1st ....26 mph @ 4100 rpm   3rd ....69 mph @ 4200 rpm
- 2nd ....42 mph @ 4100 rpm

Speedometer Error on Test Car
- Car's speedometer reading 32 48 54 65 76 86
- Weston electric speedometer ...30 45 50 60 70 80

Observed miles per hour per 1000 rpm in top gear ....23.5 mph

Stopping Distances — from 30 mph, 40 ft.; from 60 mph, 152 ft.

SPECIFICATIONS FROM MANUFACTURER

Engine
Ohv V-8
Bore: 4.0 ins.
Stroke: 3.875 ins.
Displacement: 390 cubic inches
Compression ratio: 10.5:1
Horsepower: 325 @ 4800 rpm
Ignition: 12-volt coil

Gearbox
4-speed Hydra-Matic, column control

Driveshaft
Open — 2-piece

Differential
Hypoid
Standard ratio 3.21:1

Wheels and Tires
15-in. steel disc wheels
8.20 x 15 whitewall tires

Suspension
Front: Independent upper and lower control arms; coil springs with tubular shocks and stabilizer bar
Rear: Coil springs — tubular shocks, torque being taken by control arms

Brakes
Hydraulic, servo, self-adjusting
Front and rear: 12 in. x 2.5 in. wide
Effective lining area: 203.74 sq. ins.

Body and Frame
Tubular center X
Wheelbase 129.5 ins.
Track, front 61 ins., rear 61 ins.
Overall length 222 ins.
Shipping weight 4710 lbs.

RIDING IN THE CLOSED CADILLAC IS ONE OF THE MOST SILENT EXPERIENCES ON THE ROAD TODAY. EACH YEAR THE SOUND DIMINISHES.

IMPERIAL

IN SELECTING Chrysler's Imperial LeBaron four-door Southampton hardtop, we picked the biggest of the big in the luxury field. And with LeBaron we had the top of the Imperial line — the plushest, fanciest automobile that Chrysler manufactures. We didn't have to take the measurements to realize that it is longer, wider and taller than anything else currently in the passenger car field. Massively proportioned, it looks big and impressive.

Yet, after checking exact dimensions, we found that it is only five inches longer overall than the Cadillac (actually a half-inch shorter in wheelbase), and less than two inches wider than the Cad. Its size, therefore, is partly an illusion. But only partly, as we learned while threading through narrow traffic lanes with what seemed zero clearance on the sides. So right off we were able to determine what seems to be about the only disadvantage of this car, the very thing that makes it desirable to most purchasers — its bigness. After a while, of course, the size became less noticeable and drivers compensated by driving a little less aggressively.

The modest rear window, providing considerable privacy for rear seat passengers, creates a town-car roof and a completely distinctive appearance that attracted a great deal more attention than we anticipated. Ordinarily, our domestic test cars never get a second glance, but there is something distinguished about the LeBaron that made people stare (we got the same treatment in the Rolls-Royce) — not so much at the car but at its passengers, as if onlookers were expecting to see a real live celebrity.

Actually, there have been no significant mechanical changes in the car for '62. The engine remains Chrysler's extremely potent 340-hp, 413-inch powerplant, so beloved by Chrysler owners and hot rodders alike. That much punch is not wasted; it is essential in a car that can easily scale over 6000 pounds, loaded with six passengers and luggage. At that, acceleration should please the most critical. The feeling was strong, smooth power all the way up the speed range.

The three-speed automatic transmission operates and acts just like the old TorqueFlite it replaces but it has been redesigned internally, is more compact, giving more cockpit space, and is 60 pounds lighter, due in part to an aluminum case. Shifts were perceptible but seemed exceptionally smooth, in keeping with the way we believe a luxury car should perform. One other change this year is the use of a single exhaust system instead of the duals formerly used. A single system operates hotter and should lengthen muffler and tailpipe life.

The biggest changes (for the better, we felt) have been in styling. The fins have been chopped and the rear fender line flows easily, topped by the famous gun-sight taillights. The only other appearance change worth noting is the divided grille. On the inside, everything remains as it was in '61. The instrument panel is recessed between a series of transmission and heat/cooling control pushbuttons on either side, and surmounted by a nearly square steering wheel. Its acceptance in use became a matter of personal taste. Some of the test crew liked it, others tolerated it, no one felt violently opposed to the unusual shape.

The chassis is not Chrysler's highly-touted Unibody construction. They utilize the more conventional method of heavy, box-section frame rails with body welded in place. This year they have followed the industry trend to sealed lube points so that 32,000-mile intervals between lubrications are standard.

The Imperial is brimming over with interior space, particularly in the rear seat. The distance between the rear seat backrest and the back side of the front seat can vary from 32 to 37 inches. With just over five feet of hiproom, there is plenty of area for three big adults to stretch out and be comfortable. Headroom, front and rear, 38.9/38.3 inches, is perfectly ample

THE LE BARON IS A BIG, BIG CAR AND ITS STYLISTS HAVE NOT ATTEMPTED TO HIDE THE FACT. IT HAS A REAL TOWN CAR APPEARANCE.

for tall men to sit upright. There are about 32 cubic feet in the handsomely detailed trunk. The spare, which has its own upholstered cover, mounts flat and would necessarily be buried under a full load of luggage. This is hardly a new problem and will be with us as long as spare tires are stored in trunks.

Chryslers have a reputation for good handling, and the LeBaron upheld it. Steering is quick, 3½ turns lock-to-lock, although the turning circle is an enormous 48.8 feet. While this type of car is not intended for successful hard cornering, it remained reasonably flat and controllable in turns, indicating its adaptability to mountainous terrain. Brakes, with 251 square inches of lining, stopped us moderately well from 60 mph. With more than enough power assist, required pedal pressure is very low but they showed considerable tendency to lock up, a not uncommon trait on heavy, power-braked cars.

The true feeling of luxury really came on at fast highway speeds. Cradled deeply into the soft cushions, windows closed, heating or cooling on as the climate dictated, we found the Imperial to be a magnificent road machine. There was just a slight wind rustle as it curled around the windshield chrome, but never enough to infringe upon normal conversation. Engine and road noises were effectively isolated from passengers. The ride was soft, verging on but not quite marshmallow, so that we found very little in driving or riding to contribute to fatigue.

Our test car was equipped with the optional ($57.45) limited-slip differential. We couldn't note any real advantage in normal operation although it's a handy device in snow, mud or sand. We found that the rear wheels would not break loose during our acceleration runs, which could be attributed either to the differential or the car's extreme weight.

Another option of interest is the Auto Pilot ($96.80). When locked on, it holds a steady pre-set speed over all terrain except steep downhills. Touching the brake releases it. It can be demonstrated that its use will actually increase fuel economy slightly but we found its biggest advantage on long trips, where we were able to shift position without having to worry about the position of our throttle foot.

Fuel economy is pretty much a matter of academic interest in the luxury field. The cars are big, heavy and powered with huge V-8's. What else can one expect except the eight to 12 mpg we experienced? The 2.93-to-1 axle ratio is about as far as one can practically go into an economy gear. The only answer is to keep the 23-gallon fuel tank filled.

Although it is the most expensive single option, the dual air conditioner and heater ($777.75) does an outstanding job. Temperature, heating or cooling, may be adjusted and held to precise limits and while using it we were quite unconcerned about outside weather conditions. With this type of system we found very little necessity to ever open the windows.

The extra-cost options bumped the LeBaron's price from a base of $6422 to a total of $7735.90. Destination charge added $205, making the car's delivery price $7940.90, plus tax and license. For this kind of money one expects something awfully close to the best. We can only add that anyone seeking dignified, quiet luxury really need look no further than the Imperial LeBaron.   /MT

The mammoth control console relies on the Chrysler pushbutton theme. Note the squared steering wheel.

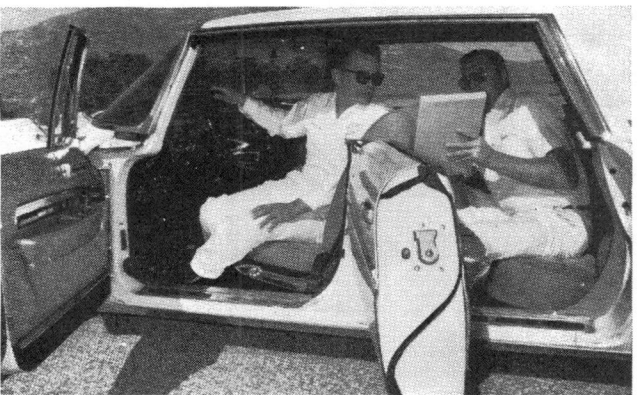

Tall men will breathe a sigh of relief when they board the Imperial. There's even hat room on the inside.

CHRYSLER IMPERIAL LE BARON
4-door, 6-passenger hardtop

OPTIONS ON CAR TESTED: Dual air conditioner and heater, Auto Pilot, Sure-Grip differential, power door locks, automatic beam changer, radio and power antenna, seat belts, tinted glass, 8.20 x 15 rayon whitewall tires, door edge protectors, remote control mirror

BASIC PRICE: $6422
PRICE AS TESTED: $7940.90 (plus tax and license)
ODOMETER READING AT START OF TEST: 4051 miles

PERFORMANCE

ACCELERATION (2 aboard)
 0-30 mph.............................. 4.2 secs.
 0-45 mph.............................. 7.1
 0-60 mph.............................. 11.0

Standing start ¼-mile 19.1 secs. and 79 mph

Speeds in gears @ shift points
 1st ......33 mph @ 3600 rpm   2nd .....75 mph @ 4000 rpm

Speedometer Error on Test Car
 Car's speedometer reading 31 49 55 65 75 85
 Weston electric speedometer ..30 45 50 60 70 80

Observed miles per hour per 1000 rpm in top gear ....24 mph

Stopping Distances — from 30 mph, 41 ft.; from 60 mph, 185 ft.

SPECIFICATIONS FROM MANUFACTURER

Engine
 Ohv V-8
 Bore: 4.19 ins.
 Stroke: 3.75 ins.
 Displacement: 413 cubic inches
 Compression ratio: 10.1:1
 Horsepower: 340 @ 4600 rpm
 Ignition: 12-volt coil

Gearbox
 3-speed automatic; dash-mounted pushbutton controls

Driveshaft
 2-piece open, pre-pack anti-friction U-joint bearings

Differential
 Standard: Hypoid, semi-floating
 Optional (test car): Sure-Grip limited-slip
 Standard ratio 2.93:1

Wheels and Tires
 Steel disc, 15 x 6 L
 8.20 x 15 rayon whitewall tires

Suspension
 Front: Independent, non-parallel control arms with torsion bars, stabilizer bar, tubular shocks
 Rear: Non-independent, semi-elliptic leaf springs, tubular shocks

Brakes
 Hydraulic, power assist; total-contact brake shoes
 Front and rear: 12 in. x 2.5 in. wide
 Effective lining area: 251 sq. ins.

Body and Frame
 Welded double-channel box-section side rails, lateral cross-members, plus X-type cross-member
 Wheelbase 129.0 ins.
 Track, front 61.7 ins., rear 62.2 ins.
 Overall length 227.1 ins.
 Shipping weight 4805 lbs.

LINCOLN CONTINENTAL

THERE IS a great temptation to describe today's Continental as a compact luxury car, and in the sense that its dimensions are substantially less than either Cadillac's or Imperial's, it is. But such a facetious tag is totally unfair, for the Continental is not really small and it measures up to accepted luxury standards in every way. And it brings to the field hidden features and a dual character that make it a surprising automobile.

We found the Continental to be loaded with quality. After making this rather obvious discovery, we dug into the manufacturing background. Lincoln is quite proud of the care they put into the car. In their second year of production on this series, they have made only minor changes for '62. They spend nearly half a car's four-day production time in inspection and testing. For example, at least once a week one of those handsome bodies is pulled off the line and destroyed, weld by weld, just to see if the various joints are holding. All engines are run on a dyno, transmissions are run for 30 minutes to check for noise and flaws and finally, each Continental gets a 12-mile road test, claimed to be the longest road check given any U.S.-built car. Obviously, they want to build a reputation, and honest quality is the best way to do it.

Styling comments are not generally part of a road test but the Continental's lines are so unusually clean and attracted such universally favorable reaction, that they deserve mention with attention to the compromises required in the interests of appearance.

Height is 53.7 inches, about three inches lower than the other two luxury cars tested, and it appears much lower, so skillfully is the roof mated with the body. A certain amount of headroom is necessarily lost. By actual measure, front/rear headroom is 33.8 and 33.6 inches. Even though the headliner is mated directly to the top, there is not a great deal of clearance for a long-torsoed individual. In fact, the Continental's graceful styling contributes to crowded quarters in one other area — the rear seat — where luxury cars usually have room to waste. Rear legroom totals 40.7, only about three inches less than the other luxury cars, but it is a significant three inches and very noticeable. Up front there is ample space, with about the same seating width, front and rear, as the other cars. As for the trunk, how big need it be? The Continental has 22.9 cubic feet, which isn't large by big-car standards. Whether it's enough depends upon the user.

We concluded that the Continental is more than a pure luxury machine — it has a definite sporting flavor. Not that it is a sports car; let's just say it's a great deal less sedate than any domestic luxury car we've ever approached and trust that sedate Continental drivers will not be offended. Even that must be qualified; it doesn't refer to performance. The Continental has the biggest engine in the field but it turns out only 300 horses, enough for good but not sensational acceleration and passing speeds. It was, however, the only luxury car that would leave rubber during a full-throttle, first-gear start.

The sports feel is a combination of several things, including interior trim, handling and ride. For one, our test car had the optional leather interior. It covers a driver's seat that has a semi-bucket effect, due to a slightly curved backrest and a soft seat section that helps hold the driver in place. Also, there was a considerable amount of chrome molding, while the headliner was of a white, perforated plastic material. Taken as a unit, these are hardly what one expects to find in a luxury car, but they were effective in lightening the somber aura that seems built into most luxury cars.

Handling was analyzed in the light of the car's intended purpose rather than in terms of cars built primarily for good handling. The Continental shaped up well, the equal of most big cars on the road, during cornering and high-speed straightaway driving. Ride struck us as the firmest in the domestic luxury field, but it was still a long way from being harsh. Bending the car hard and fast around some of the turns on the Riverside Raceway brought forth a good deal of tire protest, but the car itself remained much flatter than we expected.

THE SEMI-SPORTY CONTINENTAL WAS THE ONLY MEMBER OF THE LUXURY TRIO THAT WOULD LEAVE RUBBER ON FULL-THROTTLE ACCELERATION.

The power steering kicked back very little road feel — just enough to be helpful while cornering faster than anyone is likely to demand. The steering wheel is small, only 16 inches across, with a thin rim that is surprisingly comfortable.

There was a strong feeling of confidence in the brakes in spite of a stopping distance from 60 mph somewhat above average. They stopped straight enough, which is reassuring when trying to haul down over 5000 pounds, but wanted to lock up, hence the few extra feet of stopping caused by punching the brake pedal several times.

Various sound-deadening materials run to several hundred pounds on any luxury car, and the Continental is no exception. There was nothing to criticize adversely and little to say except that the car was very quiet; little or no wind and road noise crept in — precisely as we assumed it would be.

Lincoln is doing something with the Continental that many experts called impossible only a few years ago — building it with unit construction. It is not customary to put together a big, heavy car by this method, but it can be done, successfully. They weld the underbody, which they call a torque box, to the body. These underbody members are such heavy-gauge steel — as much as 3/16-inch thick — that they are almost a frame, but the method is unitized and Lincoln is the only luxury car builder trying it. They have proven that it works, even in their four-door convertible.

We were a little surprised to find that the big-inch V-8 is nursed along by a two-barrel carburetor. Its only possible reason for existence is economy, but that's a logical enough excuse. The Continental pulled almost 15 mpg maximum, falling to just below 10 in heavy traffic. There is one unusual engine refinement, a water-heated control for the automatic choke, which is said to aid economy during short runs. Among other things, it eliminates high engine idle speeds in short-trip operation and eliminates choke enrichment at high altitude because of low manifold vacuum pulling insufficient hot air into the choke housing.

The Continental held one more pleasant surprise — its price in relation to the luxury field. Our test car had a suggested retail of $6074, which includes a flock of extras — radio, heater, three-speed automatic transmission, power brakes, power windows, power steering, power door locks, remote control mirror and white sidewalls. Added to the price of the test car were leather interior, $100, six-way power seat at $118.95, and a fine air-conditioning system at $504.60. (This system is extremely effective and simple in its operation; it has only one knob which is also the heater control.) One can have power vent panes, electric antenna, auto pilot — in fact, every accessory available on the other two luxury cars to raise the price above the $6797.55 of our test Continental.

Staff agreement was general that Lincoln has turned out an impressive, sophisticated luxury sedan without serious faults. Since it is only the second year with a totally new design, we feel that they have done a highly commendable job in a difficult area. /MT

LINCOLN CONTINENTAL
4-door, 6-passenger sedan

OPTIONS ON CAR TESTED: Air conditioning, 6-way power seat, leather interior
BASIC PRICE: $6074
PRICE AS TESTED: $6797.55 (plus tax and license)
ODOMETER READING AT START OF TEST: 5846 miles

PERFORMANCE

ACCELERATION (2 aboard)
- 0-30 mph............................ 4.4 secs.
- 0-45 mph............................ 7.6
- 0-60 mph............................12.4

Standing start ¼-mile 19.7 secs. and 75.5 mph

Speeds in gears @ shift points
  1st ......45 mph @ 4100 rpm   2nd .....70 mph @ 4200 rpm

Speedometer Error on Test Car
  Car's speedometer reading 30 45 50 60 70 80
  Weston electric speedometer ...30 45 50 60 70 80

Observed miles per hour per 1000 rpm in top gear ....24 mph

Stopping Distances — from 30 mph, 41 ft.; from 60 mph, 205 ft.

SPECIFICATIONS FROM MANUFACTURER

Engine
  Ohv V-8
  Bore: 4.30 ins.
  Stroke: 3.70 ins.
  Displacement: 430 cubic inches
  Compression ratio: 10.0:1
  Horsepower: 300 @ 4100 rpm
  Ignition: 12-volt coil
Gearbox
  3-speed, twin-range Turbo Drive automatic; column control
Driveshaft
  Open — needle roller bearing U-joints
Differential
  Hypoid — semi-floating
  Standard ratio 2.89:1
Brakes
  Hydraulic duo-servo, self-adjusting
  Front and rear: 11.06 in. x 3 in. wide
  Effective lining area: 227 sq. ins.

Suspension
  Front: Independent with upper and lower control arms, coil springs with tubular shocks, stabilizer bar, compliance struts from front of body to lower control arms
  Rear: Non-independent, semi-elliptic leaf springs, tubular shocks
Wheels and Tires
  Pressed steel disc, 14 x 6 K
  9.50 x 14 whitewall tires
Body and Frame
  Unitized: Torque box underbody structure with welded body shell
  Wheelbase 123 ins.
  Track, front 62.1 ins., rear 61.0 ins.
  Overall length 213 ins.
  Curb weight 5132 lbs.

Front passengers are well taken care of with contoured seats, armrest and a full array of luxury components.

The Continental has the largest powerplant in the field (430 cubic inches), but turns out least power (300 hp).

Caddy Produces First New Engine in 14 Years

The casual eye will see little change for '63—but take another look

By Robert S. Ball Jr.

That roof line, with "ear muffs" at stern and smaller rear window, does little for vision, but it's the height of '63 fashion.

Instrument panel has been inched toward driver. Multiplex adapter is option with FM radio.

THE reigning monarch of U. S. luxury cars—the Cadillac, what else?—reached some sort of an anniversary last August. It turned out the last block, pistons, and accessories for an engine that it had used, with periodic modification, for 14 years. Total production in that time: a whopping 1,751,500.

When Caddy started up its factory machinery for the introduction of its 1963 models last month, it began producing a brand-new engine.

Member of the family. The new power plant was in keeping with the automobile's conservative traditions. It was still made of cast iron. It had the same displacement as its predecessor and even the same horsepower. Bore and stroke and compression ratio remained unchanged.

Then what was new in this engine, two years and more in gestation?

Two things stand out. It's lighter by several dozen pounds than last year's motor. (Cadillac engineers like to point out that the Rolls-Royce aluminum engine, seven cubic inches smaller, is actually heavier.) Second, most of the engine accessories have been regrouped in front for easier servicing.

Trimming off the fat. To lighten the engine, designers shaved nearly half an inch off the tops of the blocks, then shortened the connecting rods to keep the same compression. They cut down the length of the block by more than an inch. They hollow-cast the crankshaft, which is 11 pounds lighter than its '62 counterpart.

A switch to a 42-amp alternator-rectifier system (52 amps in the Series 75 model) saved another 10 pounds. This new unit is about the size of a heater's blower motor.

The front engine cover, the only major aluminum casting under the hood, supports the generator, steering-gear pump, distributor, oil filter, and the water, oil, and fuel pumps.

Among the virtues this adds up to is easier timing. With last year's engine, one mechanic had to turn the distributor

LOOK ALIKES are '62 and '63 Cadillac (right) but new car has many changes including double U-joints, see inset

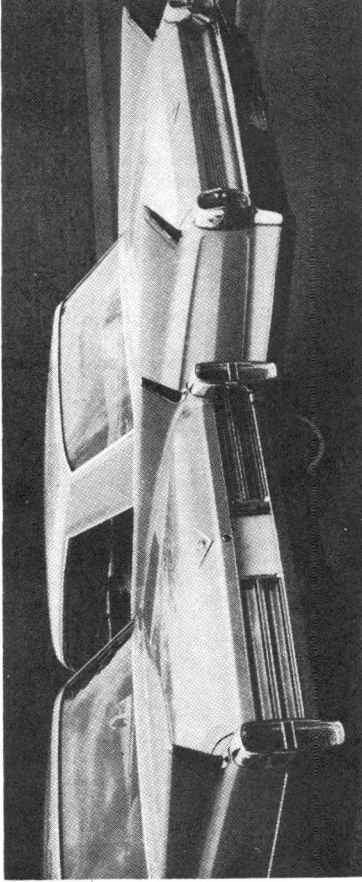

LONG LIVE THE FIN, at least the upper one which Cadillacs have worn since 1948. The 1963 car is at left

Cadillac Gets Lighter Engine, Double Universals

Cadillac stylists have an annual problem. Next year's Cadillac must look a lot like last year's, yet at the same time look brand new.

A glance at the '62 and '63 Cadillacs side by side should convince most people that the stylists have solved their problem for '63. The new car looks cleaner and crisper due principally to the removal of the "fin" that ran along the lower body of the '61 and '62, and to the switch to a straight windshield pillar.

What Cadillac calls a "modernized" engine for '63 has a new cast steel crankshaft with cored-out main bearings. The new engine is 1¼ inches shorter, but more important, 52 pounds lighter. The weight reduction is due to a new die cast aluminum front cover on which water pump, oil pump, fuel pump, distributor oil filter and steering gear pump are mounted. Bore and stroke remain 4 x 3.875 inches leaving displacement at 390 cubic inches, and horsepower at 325 is unchanged from '62.

To eliminate high speed vibration and quieten the prop shaft, Cadillac for '63 has gone to a two-piece drive shaft with double constant-velocity universal joints at the rear axle and between the two shafts, and a U-joint at the transmission. Delcotron alternators and extended life lubrication are on all models.

Cadillacs are little changed in size for 1963. Wheelbase remains at 129.5 inches on all but the series 75 limousines, while overall length generally is up an inch to 223.

inches, a compression ratio of 7.5:1—and produced all of 160 horsepower.

That engine's immediate predecessor was called the "346" after its cubage. It had a bore and stroke of 3.5 by 4.5, a compression ratio of 7.25:1—and produced 150 horsepower.

With the passing years the cubage of the 1949 engine rose to 390. The bore and stroke became over-square—4 by 3.875. The compression ratio climbed to 10.5:1, the horsepower to 325.

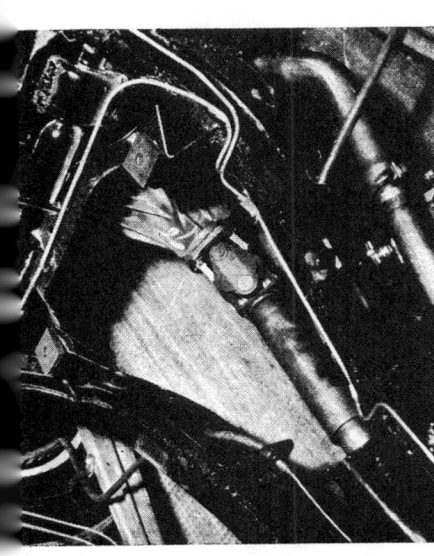

Constant-velocity joints are used at center and rear of drive shaft to reduce the slight vibration and noise set up by ordinary U joints. This is the rear one, at the differential.

(mounted toward the rear of the block) while another read the timing light.

Damping the noise. A more gimmicky innovation is the centrifugal viscous clutch on the five-bladed radiator fan used to pull air through both radiator and condenser on Cadillacs fitted with air conditioning.

Using a thermostat-controlled valve to measure out a silicone fluid between two clutch faces, the fan will barely turn at low engine speeds and low outside temperatures. It will speed up to 3,200 r.p.m. at high outside temperatures and highway speeds. The reason for keeping fan speed down: noise reduction. It also saves a bit of power.

There are other, minor modifications under the hood. The carburetor and positive crankcase-ventilation valve have been tinkered with.

In the light of today's horsepowers, Cadillac's engine of 1949 sounds, in the telling, almost like a caricature of yesteryear. It displaced 331 cubic inches, had a bore and stroke of 3.187 by 3.625

With a disdain for Detroit's now-resumed "horsepower race" that only a car of Cadillac's breeding can exhibit, the power of the new engine remains exactly the same—325.

More sprightly in the joints. For '63, Cadillac also has made significant changes in the chassis for silence and durability. Throwing cost considerations out the window, the company put two constant-velocity universal joints in the propeller shaft as well as an ordinary U joint. The CV joints are in the middle and rear of the drive shaft, the U joint just aft of the transmission.

Constant-velocity joints, by eliminating the small variations in shaft speeds in each revolution, reduce vibration and, therefore, noise.

Cadillac held up use of the CV joint for several years until long-life operation could be assured. Buick, too, employs them. Some foreign cars have used them for many years.

There is more to the Caddy's chassis
Continued on page 36

Eleven pounds lighter than last year, crankshaft is hollow-cast of heat-treated iron alloy. Main bearings are cored out to take the thicker shaft. Shorter pistons help reduce weight, too.

Caddy Produces a New Engine
CONTINUED FROM PAGE 35

refinement for the new model year. Brake cylinders have been fitted with sintered-iron pistons to fight corrosion. A backing plate has been added to the front-wheel brakes to improve sealing in wet and dusty driving. Rear-wheel bearings have special seals to retain their own lubricant.

Cadillacs are about an inch longer than last year, a fraction of an inch narrower. Wheelbase is unchanged at 129.5 inches on 60-series models, 149.8 on the 75 series.

New models are cleaner in line. Fins,

Centrifugal viscous clutch, aluminum-cast, is mounted at end of concentric shafts to save space, eliminate bearing supports. Uneven spacing of fan blades cuts high-speed noise.

first introduced by Cadillac, have receded. For what it may mean, if anything, to a change of the Caddy "image," the word "massive" is missing from the press literature.

Hood and front fenders are split-leveled in a move away from the table-tennis-court design. On two models, the Coupe de Ville and 62-series coupe, the Cinemascope rear window is gone. It's smaller. Adds prestige, they say. The instrument panel is closer to the driver.

Most interesting among the new options is an AM-FM radio, with provision for a stereo-multiplex adapter, and a six-position steering wheel. ■ ■

Cadillac presents for 1962
the Masterwork of the Motoring Age

Fleetwood Sixty Special, above; Sedan de Ville, below.

The most illustrious motor car in its distinguished sixty year history awaits your most critical inspection at the Cadillac exhibit. By any standards of judgment, you will find it the most luxurious, most superbly crafted automobile in all of motordom. However, the real test of Cadillac superiority is a demonstration drive. Your authorized dealer will arrange one at your convenience.

Cadillac Series 62 4-window sedan.

INTRODUCING THE '63 CARS

CADILLAC
Sixty, Sixty-Two & Seventy-Five

CADILLACS for 1963 will be slightly longer (about 1 in.) but slightly narrower, too (up to 0.7 in.), than they were in '62 and, like the '62s, have the same strong, solid styling. A straight, rather than curved, windshield post accentuates this feeling and the Coupe de Ville and Sixty-Two coupe have a new, shorter roofline. Padded vinyl tops also are offered, for the Coupe de Ville and Fleetwood Sixty Special. The tailfin, Cadillac says, is "tailored to present a lower profile."

Cadillac, which led the parade to overhead valve V-8s in 1949, has completely up-dated this famous engine with a complete redesign. The new engine, although the same displacement as before, is slightly smaller in overall size and 52 lb. lighter. It develops the same bhp as the '62 engine and is coupled to the same Hydra-Matic transmission. There are numerous other mechanical improvements, including an alternator, an aluminized muffler, a new drive-line with double constant-velocity joints and more safety features.

AM/FM radios are offered as optional equipment as are adjustable, tilting steering wheels. Power steering and power braking are standard equipment.

MODELS & STYLES

Sixty Series	Sixty-Two
Fleetwood	coupe
	4-window sedan
Seventy-Five	6-window sedan
limousine	convertible
sedan	Coupe de Ville
	4-window Sedan de Ville
	6-window Sedan de Ville
	Park Avenue
	Eldorado Biarritz convertible

GENERAL SPECIFICATIONS
(SIXTY-TWO 4-DOOR SEDAN)

Wheelbase, in. . . . . (Seventy-Five, 149.8). . . . 129.5
track, f & r 61.0
Overall length, in. 223.0
(Park Avenue, 215.0; Seventy-Five, 243.3)
width . . . . (Seventy-Five, 79.9). 79.7
height . . . . (Seventy-Five, 59.0). 56.4
box volume, cu. ft. . . . . (Seventy-Five, 662). 580
Luggage capacity, cu. ft. . . . . n.a.
Fuel tank capacity, gal. 26
Brakes, swept area, sq. in. 377.0
Tire size   (Seventy-Five, 8.20-15) 8.00-15
Curb weight, lb. . . . . n.a.

ENGINE

cu. in.	type	bhp/rpm	torque/rpm	carb.	comp.
390	V-8	325/4800	430/3100	1-4 bbl.	10.5

TRANSMISSION

	4th	3rd	2nd	1st	t.c.
Hydra-Matic (auto.)	1.00	1.56	2.56	3.97	—

AXLE RATIOS
Automatic transmission—2.94, 3.36, 3.77

Series 62 Coupe de Ville.

Cadillac
CROSS-COUNTRY

Cadillac's design and engineering skills produce a beautiful blend of quiet comfort, effortless performance, and flawless workmanship

MT Road Test

by Charles Nerpel, *Editor*

TAKE A CORNER of the most comfortable room in your house, add your best leather chair, float a steering wheel in your hands, imagine roadside scenery moving silently by — and you have the sensation of driving the new Cadillac.

Our 1963 Cadillac Coupe deVille test car had only 23 miles on it when we drove out of the Detroit plant, where a few days before this sporty, padded-top model had been just a series of parts numbers on a production-line chart. We did have a good chance to see MOTOR TREND's test car and others being put together on the most rigidly controlled assembly line in the United States. The pace is slower than other makers', allowing more individual attention to construction, with all major components pre-tested and adjusted before installation.

All engines, for example, have several hours of dynamometer time, running in, tuning under load, and inspection before they're put in a car. In addition, spot checks are made by grabbing engines ready for installation off the assembly line and running them again through a tear-down inspection, just to recheck previous procedures. Transmissions, brake systems, alternators — even the rear end, including differential, axles, bearings, and wheels — are also run in before assembly to the chassis.

As they leave the final production line, Cadillacs are ready to drive without a so-called break-in period. About all that's necessary for customer delivery is removal of the protective coating from the whitewall tires.

Simulated road conditions and test-running at the factory had prepared MOTOR TREND's test car, just like every Cadillac made, for regular driving immediately. We appreciated this because we drove out of the plant right smack into the thick of Detroit's metropolitan traffic. As if this baptism weren't enough for a sparkling new car, the weather was cold, and miserable rain loosened all the summer dirt into a dulling spray thrown up by passing cars. Instant heat, instant de-fogging, and a test of wipers were in order. All controls gave immediate action, with a ready flow of controllable heat, a good volume of warm, drying air over the inside windshield surface, and a wide, clean windshield pattern from the wiper blade arcs.

GM's Harrison Radiator Division, which designed the air-cooling and heating system for the Cadillac, had incorporated this unit into a complete climate control for car interiors. The refrigerated-air system and the air-heating system can be operated together, making it possible to heat refrigerated air. Unusual as this may sound, there's a noticeable difference between warm or hot air from heater control alone and warmed cooled air. Humidity under conditions of warming refrigerated air is more comfortable when outside

continued

MT'S SERIES 62 COUPE DEVILLE TEST CAR BRUSHED OFF THE RIGORS OF VARIED WEATHER AND ROAD CONDITIONS DURING 2600-MILE TRIP.

CADILLAC CROSS-COUNTRY

air is on the chilly (but not frigid) side. Of course, interior air outlets for cool and hot air are separate. When only the heater is on, warm air enters the car near the floor in the firewall area, but the regular air-conditioning outlets spew warmed cooled air when the two systems are blended. All controls for this combined interior temperature system, including high, low, and intermediate speeds for the nearly silent fan, are in one panel to the left of the steering column.

Much has been done to improve comfort in passenger cars generally, but Cadillac works at making the ultimate a reality. Seating and isolation of engine and road noises

Optional six-position steering wheel angle adjustment allows selection of desired stance while driving, ensures ample room for the stout drivers and good visibility for the short ones.

Handling ease and sure-footed stability are maintained on high-speed curves (RIGHT), without sacrificing the smooth ride and quiet comfort on the rough, gravel-covered detours (BOTTOM).

are only a part of this comfort engineering. Good temperature control and ventilation do much to lower wind noise. This plus general stability over bumps, dips, and around curves, coupled with the driver's ability to adjust himself in a position of complete ease behind the wheel, all contribute to the ultimate in comfort.

Cadillac doesn't believe in undercoating. Their engineers design for noise isolation instead of attempting to absorb or deaden existing noises inherent in a design. This isn't to say that there's *no* sound-deadening material in Cadillacs, but they do use a minimum compared to other luxury cars. Extra-size rubber bushings, designed for different cushioning rates at several impact angles, are used in all suspension pivot points. Freon-gas-filled shocks, introduced on Cadillac several years ago, are also great contributors to the car's quiet, stable operation. With this silent, non-swaying ride, devoid of the seasickening sensation once associated with such smoothness, the Series 62 has successfully combined living-room luxury with handling qualities compatible with the car's power and speed.

Power and speed are important, but the proper ratio of the power potential of the engine to performance demands is important for smooth and efficient motoring. Cadillac's new engine — lighter, smoother, and displacing 390 cubic inches — develops 325 hp at 4800 rpm. Like all engines for the full Cadillac line, this ohv, 90-degree V-8 has 10.5-to-1 (premium-fuel) compression ratio and a four-barrel carburetor. The torque output of 430 pounds-feet at 3100 rpm provides good acceleration at all speeds. Standard drive train includes the four-speed Hydra-Matic transmission and 2.94-to-1 rear-axle ratio.

Top gear gives 25 mph per 1000 rpm with 8.20 x 15 tires, but kick-down into third requires just a little extra throttle pressure even at 70 mph to provide that extra punch for shortened passing distances. The engine turns 4500 rpm in third (at 75 mph), and 4300 rpm produces 25 mph in first and 40 mph in second. Two settings for DRIVE allow quadrant selection to hold the Hydra-Matic in third for engine braking or to reduce automatic downshifting from fourth to third in heavy traffic.

The engine itself, all new for 1963, is one inch lower, four inches narrower, and 1¼ inches shorter than last year's powerplant. It adds up to a weight saving of nearly 52 pounds. Water pump, oil and fuel pumps, distributor, oil filter, and power steering pump are grouped together on a die-cast aluminum cover on the front of the engine — a great aid for easier servicing of these important components. Also helping performance and durability are the cast Armasteel crankshaft and cored-out main bearings of larger diameter for lighter weight and better wear characteristics — this plus shorter, lighter pistons.

Added weight reduction and improved electrical power output are provided by the Delcotron alternator, standard for '63. The normal unit has a 45-ampere output, but cars equipped with air-conditioning systems come with a 52-ampere unit. Even the five-bladed fan is alloy on air-conditioned cars, and it has a sensing device to maintain maximum efficiency for both speed and temperature.

Drive line noise, a big concern with most designers, has been virtually eliminated by using a split driveshaft, divided by a double, constant-velocity universal joint. Utilizing a

Rear seat has a folding center arm rest that doesn't interfere with the center seat back comfort when stowed.

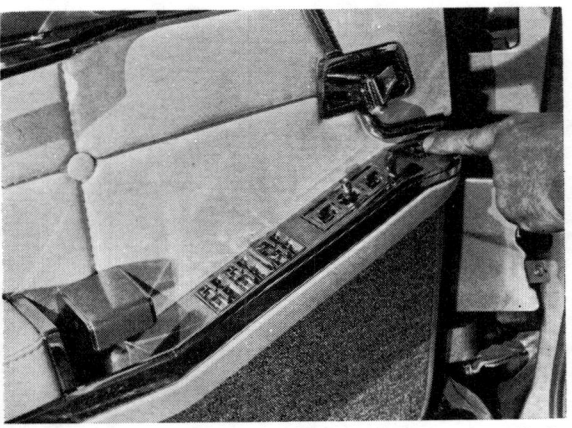

Electric control console on driver's door groups all the switches for windows, windwings, seats, and door locks into one convenient location for fingertip operation.

Bench-type front seat (bucket seats are optional) has a center folding arm rest, well padded and wide enough for both driver and passenger. Both front seat backs can be tilted forward for easy rear seat access.

CADILLAC CROSS-COUNTRY
continued

HEADING SOUTH IN THE CRISP, COLD DAWN, CADILLAC'S INTERIOR COMFORT FEATURES AND CLIMATE CONTROL MAKE DRIVING A PLEASURE.

front shaft anchored near the center, the relatively short rear section of this drive line is practically insensitive to heavy passenger or luggage loads.

Body design of the Coupe deVille is very interesting, especially the roof. Over the regular steel top is a layer of insulated padding, and covering this is cross-grain vinyl. The result is a smooth line, with the sporty look of a padded-top convertible. We believe that much of the silent ride and most of the air conditioning and heating efficiency are due to the pleasing roof material. It deadens noise and insulates against heat and cold.

Other styling changes for 1963 include a completely new front-end treatment, plus new hood sheet metal. A close look at this shape reveals a striking similarity to last year's rear deck lid, turned around of course, so that the lateral crease is forward. In addition, the ventral fins that ran along the lower rear fenders have been eliminated, smoothing the entire rear end and making the upper fins less conspicuous. Stop lights, combined with turn signals in the rear, are more noticeable when separated from the regular tail light system. Front lighting, using quad lamps, has been designed into the slight separate-fender-from-body style, and last year's curb light for illuminating the blind spot just outboard of the headlight beam has been retained and improved. This light, which comes on when the turn signal is actuated, is a valuable driving aid for maneuvering into dark, narrow areas.

On the road or in traffic, driving the Cadillac is a pleasure. Fingertip electric adjustment of the seat through a wide range of height, distance, and tilt, plus six different steering wheel settings, puts any driver in a near-perfect stance to handle this 129-inch-wheelbase car as if it were a compact.

Driving position probably has more to do with the feeling of the size of a car than anything else. Small cars with high steering wheels, low seats, and great seat-to-pedal distance can and do give smaller drivers the feeling they're driving a truck. Cadillac adjustments, on the other hand, provide even the short driver with a position of visibility and ease not ordinarily associated with cars nearly 19 feet long.

This same lightness and sure-footed control are best noted on expressways and turnpikes, some of which now have legal speeds up to 75 or 80 mph. Route 66, under its present conditions of divided super-highway, stretches under construction, and about-to-be-abandoned parts of the "old" highway, gives just about every type of touring anyone's likely to find on a cross-country trip. Handling on curves and in the wet is firm, and the optional limited-slip differential shows its advantages in the loose gravel of detours.

Braking is superb, with a double system that still assures either forward or rear wheel braking, should one or the other half fail through line fracture or other mishap. All in all, cross-country touring in a Cadillac is like a conducted tour in your own private floating compartment. /MT

All-new engine is smaller, lighter, smoother, and more rugged, with major serviceable components more accessible for repair or adjustment. New feature is the lightweight Delcotron alternator.

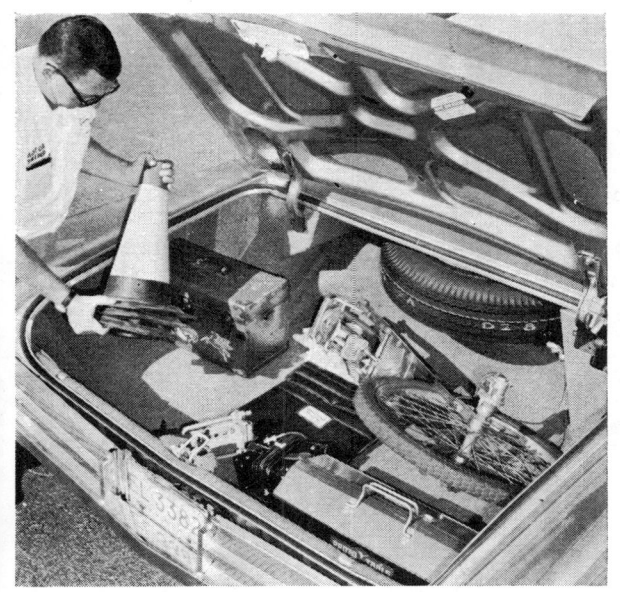

More usable luggage space is available through location of spare in seldom-used area over the rear axle body hump.

Cast iron drums with cooling fins house self-adjusting shoes. Hydraulic cylinders operated by dual master unit have new long-wearing, sintered-iron pistons.

The optional cruise control mounted on cowl can maintain constant speed on either level or hills. A touch of the brake pedal unlocks the system.

1963 CADILLAC SERIES 62 COUPE DE VILLE
2-door, 6-passenger sedan

OPTIONS ON CAR TESTED: Air conditioning, AM-FM radio, controlled differential, adjustable steering wheel, power headlight control, cruise control, power seat control

BASIC PRICE: $5386
ODOMETER READING AT START OF TEST: 23 miles
RECOMMENDED ENGINE RED LINE: 5000 rpm

PERFORMANCE

ACCELERATION (2 aboard)
0-30 mph	3.6 secs.
0-45 mph	6.4
0-60 mph	10.4

Standing start ¼-mile 19 secs. and 81 mph
Speeds in gears @ shift points
   1st ......25 mph @ 4300 rpm
   2nd ......40 mph @ 4300 rpm
   3rd ......75 mph @ 4500 rpm

Speedometer Error on Test Car
  Car's speedometer reading 30 45 50 60 71 81
  Weston electric speedometer ..30 45 50 60 70 80
Observed miles per hour per 1000 rpm in top gear ....25 mph
Stopping Distances — from 30 mph, 40 ft.; from 60 mph, 156 ft.

SPECIFICATIONS FROM MANUFACTURER

Engine
90-degree ohv V-8
Bore: 4.0 ins.
Stroke: 3.875 ins.
Displacement: 390 cubic inches
Compression ratio: 10.5:1
Horsepower: 325 @ 4800 rpm
Torque: 430 lbs.-ft. @ 3100 rpm
Horsepower per cubic inch: 0.83
Ignition: 12-volt coil

Gearbox
Hydra-Matic 4-speed automatic; quadrant selector

Driveshaft
Two-piece, open tube, with double constant-velocity joint

Differential
Ring and pinion — limited-slip
Standard ratio: 2.94:1

Suspension
Front: Independent, with coil springs, tubular shocks, stabilizer bar
Rear: Solid axle; 4-link stabilizer, coil springs, tubular shocks

Steering
Ball nut sector, with in-line hydraulic power
Turning diameter: 43 ft.
Turns: 3.7 lock to lock

Wheels and Tires
15-inch slotted steel disc wheels
8.20 x 15 tires

Brakes
Hydraulic drum; servo, self-adjusting
Front: 12-in. composite cast iron — finned
Rear: 12-in. composite cast iron — finned
Effective lining area: 221.8 sq. ins.

Body and Frame
Separate steel body on X-member frame
Wheelbase: 129.5 ins.
Track: front, 61 ins.; rear, 61 ins.
Overall length: 223.0 ins.
Shipping weight: 4750 lbs.

43

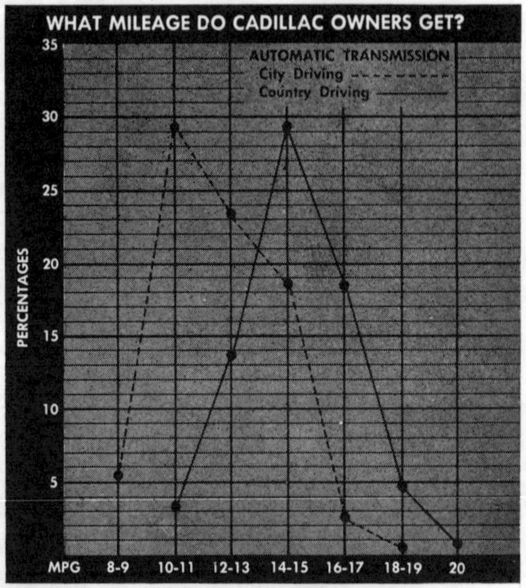

Cadillac Owners Praise Handling Comfort, Find Ash Trays Distressing

A Nationwide Survey Based on 905,927 Owner-Driven Miles

Marginal and boldface comments by Jim Whipple, *PM's* Automotive Editor

CURIOSITY prompted *PM's* choice of Cadillac as a subject for an owners report. The car has been the unchallenged leader of its class for years and currently outsells its two domestic competitors *combined* by a three-to-one margin.

Although it is priced at less than half the cost of a Rolls Royce, Cadillac has become a world-wide symbol of a top-quality motor car. It is equally esteemed by Arabian sheiks, Argentine cattle barons and American bankers.

But why do these—and others—choose Cadillac? Although it sounds almost absurd, the reason that most people buy Cadillacs is simply because the car is a Cadillac. For example, 77.1 percent traded another Cadillac for this year's model, and 78 percent cited previous ownership as a primary reason for buying.

Of the entire group responding, a whopping 75.8 percent stated that they did not consider buying another luxury car. Of the 24.2 percent who did consider another car before buying their Cadillacs, 55.6 percent considered the Lincoln Continental, 16.7 percent looked at the big Buick, 11.1 percent considered the Imperial, and Thunderbird. And an overwhelming 98.7 percent stated that they

Can you think of another car with a play on Broadway like the "Solid Gold Cadillac?"

Cadillac management has shrewdly resisted temptation to overproduce for quick profits, thus they always have an order backlog and used models remain high in value

ELEGANCE OF CADILLAC STYLING was mentioned by over half the owners surveyed as a major factor in their decision to buy the General Motors luxury car

BEGINNING WITH THE P-38 LOOK right after World War II, Cadillac originated tail fins in the domestic market. They're lower now, but they won't die

MORE CITY DRIVERS got a fuel consumption rate of 10 miles per gallon than any other. On the open road, 15 miles per gallon was the most common figure

Owners Like... But Dislike

Comfort, Luxury Ride (52.0%)   Ash Trays (9.9%)
Easy Handling (38.1%)   Inadequate Heater (7.2%)
Power, Performance (33.6%)   Whistling Wind (4.9%)

44

In no other owners report has reputation played so important a role in determining a purchase →

People seem to look for these qualities no matter what car they buy →

Cadillac owners are not fusspots. Those '63 ash trays are a comedy of errors →

That four-speed Hydra-Matic transmission and the 2.94 rear-axle ratio are what make the heavy Cad so surprisingly thrifty →

Note similar mileage at 30 and 50 m.p.h.; it's due to transmission characteristics making 50 a very economical cruising speed →

did *not* consider an imported luxury car which we assume would include such makes as Rolls Royce, Mercedes Benz and Jaguar.

In addition to previous ownership other important reasons given by owners for their purchases were comfort (62.3 percent), reputation (58.3 percent) and styling (54.3 percent). (Note that these are overlapping percentages.)

After driving their Cadillacs for an average of 4175 miles, the owners checked off as their Best Liked features, a list surprisingly similar to that of a group of low-priced car owners. The top four were Riding Comfort, Handling Ease, Performance and Styling in that order.

Some 46.2 percent of all owners reporting had no complaints whatsoever. Topping the list of what complaints there were was the location of ash trays. This is something of a left-handed compliment; a car must be pretty good if its major fault is misplaced ash trays.

Fuel economy would not seem to be important to owners of a luxury car costing over $6000, but Cadillac owners are aware of the degree of thirst of their cars.

A solid 69.1 percent felt that their Cadillacs were delivering about the mileage expected, which for most drivers ran between 10 and 14 miles per gallon in city traffic and from 12 to 17 miles per gallon on the open roads.

As a check, and for comparison with other cars, *PM* ran constant speed fuel mileages with a fuel meter on its test Cadillac. The car, a Coupe de Ville hardtop, had a full complement of power accessories including air conditioning. It delivered these fuel mileages:

19.83 miles per gallon at 30 m.p.h.
22.85 miles per gallon at 40 m.p.h.
19.18 miles per gallon at 50 m.p.h.
17.53 miles per gallon at 60 m.p.h.
15.65 miles per gallon at 70 m.p.h.

Over-all fuel consumption for approximately 850 miles of driving, about 40 percent of which was in city traffic, worked out to 14.9 miles per gallon.

The owners rated their Cadillacs high with 76.2 percent stating that the cars were excellent, while 20.6 percent felt that they were good. Only 1.4 percent of those reporting categorized their Cadillacs as fair, while 1.8 rated them as poor.

One sure proof of a car's worth is the inclination of its owners to buy another one of the same make. Cadillac owners made it almost unanimous with 91.4 percent of all the owners reporting that they would buy again.

Of the remaining 8.6 percent, 6.8 percent was undecided while 1.8 percent said that they would not buy another Cadillac.

What do the owners themselves say about their Cadillacs? Here, from the affirmative comments made, are the five that were mentioned most often:

"Rides well on both bumpy roads and smooth pavements."—New York restaurant owner.

"I like the driving comfort and lack of fatigue after a long drive."—Iowa surgeon.

"It's easy handling for its size."—New Jersey housewife.

"It's just like driving a cloud—practically effortless!"—New Jersey salesman.

"A nice running and easily handled automobile."—Illinois steamship agent.

"My Cadillac handles very well at all speeds."—Indiana doctor.

"Like its precision in handling."—New York clergyman.

"I like its smooth, quick acceleration."—Pennsylvania merchant.

"Has speed when needed."—New York sales engineer.

"I like the simplicity of styling; they've eliminated the

PM testers found Cadillac's ride generally superior, although on bad washboard surfaces there was some muffled vibration from the massive unsprung rear wheel and axle assembly →

Let's put it this way: If clouds were equipped with power steering, they'd handle like Cadillacs!

← *Steering is precise and the car goes exactly where you point it. But some drivers may feel that the steering is a bit too light and easy*

SUMMARY OF OWNERS REPORT

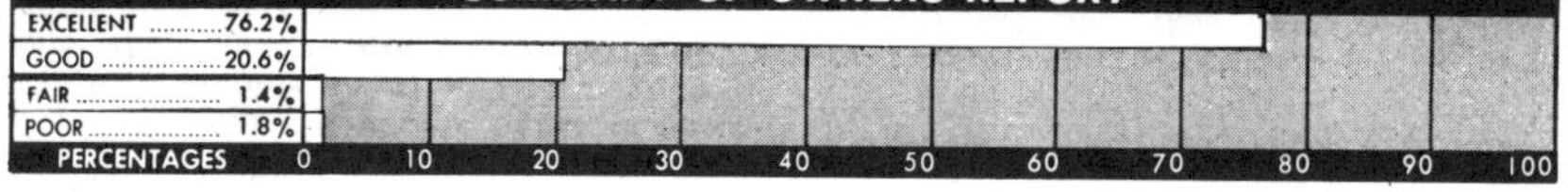

PERCENTAGES	0–100
EXCELLENT	76.2%
GOOD	20.6%
FAIR	1.4%
POOR	1.8%

Category	%
Mileage experience	
About as expected	69.1%
Better	14.5
Not as good	16.4
Best-liked features	
Riding comfort	52.0
Handling ease	38.1
Power, performance	33.6
Styling	31.4
Smooth, quiet	10.3
Roominess	6.7
Adequate headroom	6.3
Specific complaints	
Location of ash trays	9.9
Inadequate heater	7.2
Wind noise	4.9
Doors, windows fit poorly	4.0
Mechanical trouble if any	
No mechanical trouble	76.7
Excessive oil consumption	3.1
Defective oil seal	1.8
Windshield wipers	1.8
Fast engine idle	1.8
Best-liked exterior style features	
Clean, smooth look	10.8
Simple, plain, classic lines	9.0
Lower fins	6.3
Hood	4.5
Grille	4.0
Small rear window	4.0
Long, low lines	3.6
Front end	3.6
Least-liked exterior style features	
Rear window	4.5%
Fins	4.0
Fenders	2.7
Length	1.8
Grille	1.8
Vulnerable front end	1.3
No protective molding	1.3
Plain, undistinguished	1.3
Best-liked interior style features	
Dashboard	13.0
Upholstery	12.6
Comfortable seats	10.3
Adjustable seats	3.6
Arm rests	2.7
Legroom	2.2
Color harmony	2.2
Luxurious, quality look	2.2
Interior lighting	1.8
Least-liked interior style features	
Ash trays	9.0
Transmission hump	5.4
Glove compartment	4.0
Upholstery	3.6
Uncomfortable seats	3.1
Dashboard	2.2
Interior lighting	2.2
Decision to buy Cadillac most influenced by:	
Previous ownership	78.0
Comfort	62.3
Reputation	58.3
Consider buying another luxury car?	
Yes	75.8%
Did not consider	24.2
What make?	
Lincoln Continental	55.6
Imperial	11.1
Buick	16.7
Consider An Imported Luxury Car?	
Did not consider	98.7
Did consider	1.3
Make of family's other car, if any	
No other car	4.7
Another Cadillac	19.7
Chevrolet	5.4
General Motors compacts	9.0
Other General Motors make	10.8
Ford	1.8
Ford Motor compacts	3.1
Other Ford Motor make	0.9
Chrysler Corp. compacts	4.5
Other Chrysler Corp. make	5.4
Other U.S. make	5.4
How is dealer service?	
Excellent	60.5
Average	36.6
Poor	3.2
Would you buy from him again?	
Yes, would buy again	68.1
No, would not	4.5
Would you buy another Cadillac?	
Yes, would buy	91.4
No, would not buy	1.0

THE CAVERNOUS CADILLAC TRUNK is even equipped with a neatly painted wooden wedge to block a wheel in the unhappy event that you get a flat tire

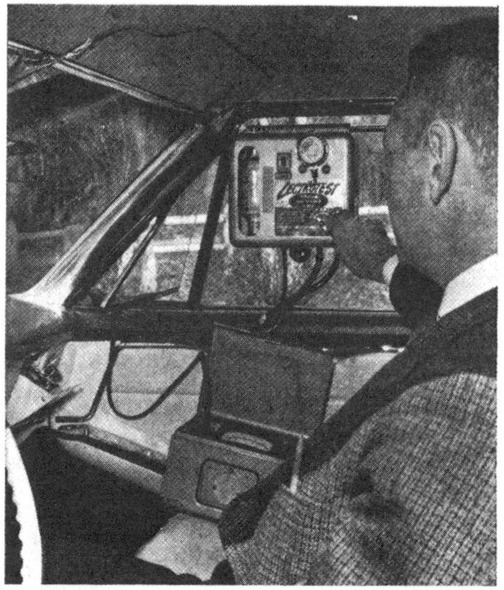

PM'S FUEL METER REPORTED steady-speed economy up to 22.85 miles per gallon, but weight—nearly three tons—keeps owners' highway results under 20 m.p.g.

45

heavy, bulky appearance."—Connecticut labor union official.

Each year Cadillac's design grows a bit more tasteful and refined—more like a "gentleman's carriage", less like a space ship.

"Good general appearance—it's not ornate," Michigan sales manager.

"I like most its over-all length and streamlined appearance."—Ohio clerical worker.

A couple of years ago Cadillac offered a "compact" model with seven inches lopped off the trunk. It sold like a Valentine card on the 15th of February.

"Like the clean lines from front to rear."—New York investigator.

"The car has an all-around quality that makes for pleasant operation."—Washington retiree.

"It's the smoothest of the four different cars I've owned."—Ohio physician.

In normal driving Cadillac goes like a velvet canoe in a lake of pure cream.

Corresponding negative comments also were made, of course. Here, in the order of their frequency, are the five most often recorded:

"Do not like the dash ash tray; driver's side not illuminated."—Ohio executive.

"I wish the ash trays were better located and larger."—Arkansas investment counselor.

Most '63 Cadillac drivers would agree. The left front tray (and lighter) is so low that driver must take eyes from the road completely; at night it is unlighted so ashes land in trouser cuff, butts go out the window and tray can only be found when you move right foot—then your knee hits it. Only possible conclusion is that Cadillac ash trays must have been designed by a non-smoker.

"Put the ash tray where it was in the '62 model."—Michigan executive.

"Ash trays difficult to open and midget-sized glove compartment, likewise."—California grain dealer.

On PM's test car the Auto Editor's wife broke a fingernail trying to get into flush-door right-hand tray.

"Heating system is too slow."—Illinois executive.

"On cars having air conditioning, there is no arrangement for getting fresh air into the car without having the air conditioner or heater on, or having a window open, and there are many times when neither of these is desirable."—Florida retiree.

Efforts to "simplify" Cadillac heater controls have gone awry, but completely! You cannot get either hot or cold air without using blower, and car is so tightly sealed that you need top blower speed to demist windshield.

"Heater fan and heater controls should be on right side of steering wheel."—Ohio retiree.

"Defrosters do not heat the bottom of the windshield, so snow sticks at the bottom."—New York restaurant owner.

"There's too much wind noise from wind wings—one cannot even hear the radio or talk."—California contractor.

One of the problems of making a truly quiet running car—little noises become big nuisances. Incidentally the radio (AM-FM) has great tonal quality. What this car needs most is a means of getting a large volume of fresh air into and out of the body quietly.

"Poorly fitting doors and windows which cause whistling noise."—Ohio executive. "It uses too much oil."—Tennessee pharmacist.

Returning to the bright side, here are numbers 6 through 10 of the praiseworthy points Cadillac owners mentioned. They're listed in the order of their frequency:

"Plenty of space for family travel."—Illinois factory representative.

"It's easy to get into, has good headroom."—New Jersey sales engineer.

Front and rear headroom dimensions are above average on '63 Cadillac.

"I like the higher top; it's easy for a tall person to ride without striking head."—Connecticut retiree.

"I like the convenience and dependability of the Cadillac."—Alabama accountant.

"Like the tip-up steering wheel."—New York physician.

It offers a worthwhile change of position, but the six-way power seat is much more important to driver comfort.

"I like the '63 model better than the '60. It has more headroom and better visibility when in traffic."—New York executive.

Large glass areas and sharply defined "corners" of the car make close-quarter driving less of a problem than you'd expect with a car this size.

"I like the performance, comfort and visibility."—New Jersey contractor.

For each bit of praise, some owner has a corresponding comment about something that disappointed him. Following are numbers six through 10 of the shortcomings noted:

"Very, very poor paint job over-all."—Michigan retiree.

"Poor paint job; they didn't tape up the white top when painting body."—Arizona doctor.

At $6000-plus, the paint job should be perfect on every single car.

"Selection of seat upholstery the worst in years. Cadillac buyers are entitled to much better."—Michigan retiree.

"It seems to me that the interiors are less attractive on each model I buy, and I have owned seven to date."—Nebraska retiree.

"Upholstery is not top quality."—South Carolina physician.

If you consider top quality equal to the grade of materials used in the $16,000 import whose initials are RR, you'd have to agree with the doctor.

"Body interior quality not as good as it should have been."—Michigan retiree. "'Ford' hardtop styling cuts down essential visibility toward rear of vehicle."—Indiana advertising executive.

He's right, of course, but this "blind rear quarter" styling originated on T-Bird, is the hottest thing in styling since fins went back to the fish.

"It should get better gas mileage compared to other Cadillacs I've had; I only get 12 to 14 m.p.g."—California businessman.

"It uses too much gas, but this was expected."—California housewife.

"It's too noisy for a luxury car."—Connecticut pharmacist.

"Elimination of dual exhaust makes motor exhaust much noisier. I miss the quietness of the 1960 Cadillac."—California court reporter.

To wind up the enthusiastic statements by Cadillac owners, here are comments number 11 through 16 on the good side:

"The workmanship is excellent."—Michigan self-employed man.

There are three reasons for this: 1) conservative engineering, 2) time, 3) money.

"No annoying mechanical adjustments required."—California food wholesaler.

"Cadillac has the reputation and 'Fort Knox' association I enjoy and appreciate."—Ohio business speech teacher.

"What I consider very important is the trade-in value." New York banker.

Thousands of people have listed their names with Cadillac dealers waiting for carefully tended two or three-year old Cads to be traded.

"Holds the road better than previous year models."—Florida housewife.

"It drives well in snow because it's well-weighted."—New Jersey attorney.

"I like the adjustable brakes."—Colorado fire fighter.

"I also like the emergency brake release."—Texas executive.

This feature is great. When you move gear selector from Neutral to Drive, parking brake is automatically released.

"It's economical for a large car."—New Jersey physician.

It never ceases to surprise people, PM staff included, when they get 16 to 17 miles per gallon on the road in a Cadillac that weighs two and one-half tons.

Numbers 11 through 16 of the adverse owner comments wrap up negative reactions to the '63 Cadillac owners report:

"Inside rear view mirror is not in correct position for a tall person. I consider it dangerous."—Wisconsin dentist.

"The inside rear-view mirror is placed too low giving you a blind spot through the windshield."—Michigan plumber.

On a car in Cadillac's bracket, vertical adjustment of the mirror should be a matter of course.

"There are rattles indicating poor production supervision."—Illinois city mayor.

"I don't believe the factory inspection at delivery time is thorough enough, for they have passed motor noises and final adjustments in general on to owner who has to appeal to dealer for correction—easier said than done."—Ohio housewife.

"Had electrical failure of windshield wipers."—Colorado dentist.

"The roof is too low—hits my hat when I get in and out."—Minnesota traveling salesman.

"People continually scraping knees as ashtrays open by themselves and have sharp edges."—New York bakery owner.

This completes the roll call of owners' pros and cons on their 1963 Cadillacs based on a combined experience of 905,927 miles driven. ★★★

'64 Cadillac Makes Its Own Weather

Some styling changes, a bigger engine, and a new drive for more zip in the passing ranges also make news in this luxury car

Styling changes include new grille, lower tail fins.

ONE day last June, Dan Adams, Cadillac's assistant chief engineer, fired up a test automobile on the streets of Denver, then moved a knob on his instrument panel until an arrow on it pointed at 72. That meant degrees of temperature.

Beside Adams was a fellow engineer. The day was bright, the outside air at 85 degrees. In a matter of minutes, with the windows rolled up, a thermometer in the car read exactly what Adams had asked for—72 degrees.

They started driving west. An hour and a half later they were in the middle of a snowstorm in the Rockies' Loveland Pass. The outside temperature had dropped 50 degrees to just above freezing. But the thermometer stayed right where it had been at the start, 72 degrees.

Last month, when Cadillac announced its 1964 models, a dial-your-weather system, called Comfort Control, was a prominent option. Comfort Control had been a long time in incubation. Cadillac started experimenting with dial-your-weather five years ago. The goal was complete freedom from adjustment of the heater and air-conditioner. When, last year, the engineers combined the heating-cooling systems, they were well on their way.

Giving Nature a hand. Comfort Control is based on the premise that the human body is the world's worst thermostat. It reacts slowly to small changes in temperature. The motorist, fiddling with his heater or air-conditioning controls, may overadjust, because he's let car temperature get way out of the comfort zone. Cadillac uses electric sensors to "read" all car conditions affecting comfort. The result is the world's first wholly automatic inside-weather system for cars, or, for that matter, for anything else.

For an explanation of how Comfort Control works, see diagram on page 66. Cadillac has other things for '64. In only its third boost in engine displacement in 14 years, the company has added 39 cubic inches for a total of 429. The bigger engine is combined in some of the new Cadillacs—about three out of every five coming off the assembly line—with a new transmission called the Turbo Hydra-Matic. And this is the first basic change in transmissions for Cadillac since 1940.

Zip and economy. In a car weighing almost 4,800 pounds, engine and transmission provide quite an improvement in performance. Zero to 60 miles an hour has been chopped from 12 to 10.2 seconds. The car has a third more torque for passing at 50 m.p.h., twice as much at 20 m.p.h. Astonishingly, Cadillac's gas economy hasn't been affected.

A couple of gadgets should please the absentminded: an electric eye that turns on the headlights at twilight and a time-delay switch that automatically turns the headlights off a couple of minutes after the car has been parked for the night.

But the big thing for the new model year is that Comfort Control. Any bragging that Cadillac does about it is characteristically conservative. "The inside temperature may vary plus or minus a degree or so from the setting," says Dan Adams with an engineer's preciseness. I say your home thermostat should be so good!—*Devon Francis.*

Electric eye for automatic headlight dimmer is moved from dash to tip of front fender. Horsepower is upped from 325 to 340. Fifteen years ago Cadillac boasted a whopping 160 hp.

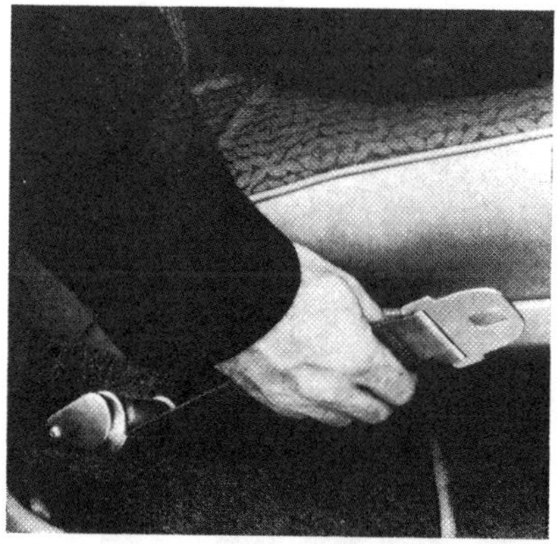

Seat belt ends have a spring-loaded retracter. Tiltable steering wheel, introduced last year, now has seven instead of six positions. Leather seat trim is perforated for ventilation.

Cadillac's "ducks" aren't ducks

Those things that look like ducks on the famous Cadillac crest aren't. Part of the design since 1904, they are "merlettes"—birds that never existed—ancient heraldic symbols of knighthood. They are legless and beakless. Appearing in threes, and considered sacred to the Holy Trinity, they were granted by the School of Heralds to knights for valiant conduct in the Crusades.

The Exciting '64s!

REVISED parking lamp location marks the '64 Cadillac. New lamp is behind small grille.

CADILLAC, WHICH produced a new V-8 engine for last year's cars, has bored and stroked that engine to more competitively power its 1964s. Teaming this engine with a new automatic transmission, plus further automating various comfort and convenience accessories, makes the mechanical developments overshadow the styling refinements at this GM division.

With 0.125 in. added to the bore, and with a longer stroke (now 4.13 by 4.0 in.), displacement has been increased from 390 to 429 cu. in. The 10% increase in capacity, together with slightly altered cam configuration, increases output to 340 bhp at 4600 rpm and torque to 480 lb./ft. at 3000 rpm.

The new transmission, a combination of Hydra-Matic and torque converter called Turbo Hydra-Matic, is used in the de Ville series, the 60 Special Sedan and Eldorado (sans Biarritz) convertible. The 62 series and Fleetwood 75 sedan and limousine retain the older Hydra-Matic transmission, which also has undergone some engineering changes to increase cooling and, in commercial units, to beef up the reverse unit.

Shift lever pattern, in keeping with the trend, is PRNDL, which requires different shifting habits between series (H-M pattern is PNDDLR). To remind multi-Cadillac owners that reverse is engaged by pushing up on the lever rather than pulling down, a different shift lever knob is installed with the Turbo Hydra-Matic transmission. It can be downshifted to 2nd at speeds between 20-60 mph to provide engine braking on hills. Since the torque converter aids all gears, the transmission doesn't have "blank spots" where vehicle speed is too high for one gear and too low for another; it also performs with more agility in the city traffic range of 20-45 mph. The new unit weighs 30 lb. less than the old Hydra-Matic.

A new speedometer drive provision has four different worm gears and six different pinions available to more closely calibrate the speedometer to the vehicle weight, tire size and gearing. An iron spacer between engine and transmission to accommodate two different bolt hole patterns is the clue to this transmission's interchangeability with Buick.

Electronics have moved further into Cadillac's accessory field, with a thermostatically operated comfort control which combines the heater and air conditioner. This automatically warms,

Cadillac Series 60

FLEETWOOD ELDORADO convertible shows 1 in. lower fins for '64, plus slightly modified grille. New 429-cu.in. engine will power all Cadillac models.

cools, or blends air—all through a dehumidifier—on demand from a sensing valve to maintain a constant temperature within the car.

Another optional device is the Twilight Sentinel, operated by three photo cells, which automatically turns on headlights at dusk, turns them off at dawn, so long as the engine is running. The control is adjustable for sensitivity and has a delayed action which will keep headlights on for up to 90 sec. after the ignition is switched off. A de-activator switch has been added to the power window circuit, permitting the driver to cut off each individual window switch for safety reasons. The automatic headlight dimming photo cell has been moved to the left headlight hood, where it is styled into the trim strip. A factory-installed rear window de-fogger is offered and the tilting steering wheel now adjusts to seven positions.

As befits a motor carriage considered the height of luxury by many Americans, there are 124 upholstery options available, including 4 standard and 15 optional leather colors (perforated or plain). The Eldorado and Fleetwoods have simulated wood veneer panels as part of the interior trim. Exterior restyling includes lowering the tail fin 1 in., flattening the deck lid between the tail fins, bringing the grille forward more on a single plane between front fenders and dividing it with a strip in body paint color. Relocating the spare tire above the rear axle results in a deeper trunk well and greater usable luggage space. ∎

POPULAR DE VILLE series will have two 4-door hardtops (4-window at left, 6-window above) and 2-door hardtop coupe (below). All will have new Turbo Hydra-Matic transmission as standard equipment.

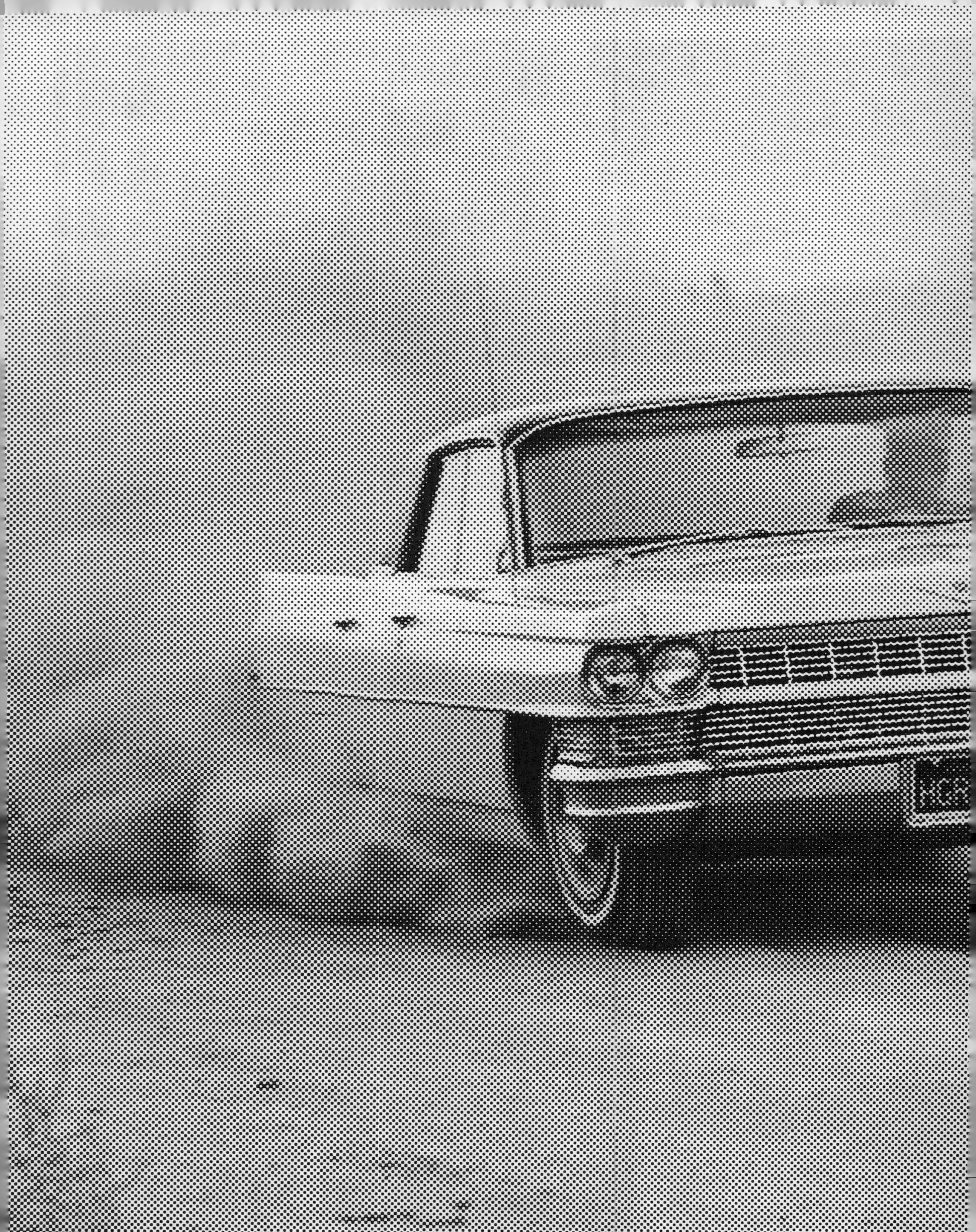

Cadillac
SEDAN DE VILLE
MT ROAD TEST

by Jim Wright, *Technical Editor*

EVERY YEAR, Cadillac seems to turn out the standard for the luxury field — the car to beat. So far no one has beat it or even come close. Cadillac sales for 1963 will close out right at 160,000 units (probably more for '64). This means almost five times as many Cads will have been sold for the year as its two domestic competitors combined. After driving and evaluating all of them, including the choice European models, it isn't hard to understand why. On a straight dollar-value basis, none of the other luxury models offers quite what the Cadillac does in terms of quality, comfort, and overall performance. Most lack the interior roominess, too.

Some imported models have the quality by virtue of their hand fitting. But if these European manufacturers could find a way to *profitably* tool up for mass production, they'd do it. The comfort is there, too. But then, even the lowest-priced luxury imports cost at least twice as much as a Cadillac, and you'd have to beat us with a large club to convince us that they're that much better — if at all. When it comes to overall performance (including handling and roadability), the imports aren't equal, though some excel in individual aspects.

Of domestic luxury cars, the competition is in the same price range, and it's strictly a matter of opinion in judging their quality and comfort factors. When it comes to overall performance, we have to go by the results of our tests, and these tell us the Caddy is unequalled by anything at any price.

Our test car, a four-window, four-door Sedan de Ville, had a little over 800 miles on it when we picked it up. Even if the mileage had been zero, the test car would still have been ready for anything, because all Cads are run in at the factory and don't need a break-in. Our test car was loaded with every major accessory available. This is the way most of them are ordered (65 per cent with air conditioning), and in addition to checking out the car, we also wanted to check all the creature comforts. Standing at the curb with a full

Cadillac's famous fin, still very much in evidence, was lowered an inch this year.

Just above headlights, in chrome decoration, stands sensor for automatic dimmer.

Tail lights, bumpers, and grille are massive, but otherwise trim use is minimal.

CADILLAC SEDAN DE VILLE *continued*

tank of gas (26 gallons), our test car weighed in at a not-so-modest 5050 pounds. And if there's ever been anything this big that'll move as fast, we haven't heard of it.

As you can see from the acceleration tables, it's going to take a hot-option model of anything else to stay with this one from a standing start. Our '64 times are also quite a bit faster than the '63 times. This is due to the redesigned and enlarged engine *and* the new torque-converter transmission.

The bigger engine is the result of both bore and stroke increases. With displacement now at 429 cubic inches, the '64 Cadillac engine is one of the two biggest in the industry. Horsepower has been increased from 325 to 340 (at 4600 rpm), and the torque rating is now 480 pounds-feet at 3000 rpm. Incidentally, this torque figure is equal to what the big Super/Stock engines are putting out and does a lot to explain the rapid acceleration and pulling power of the Cadillac.

The new Turbo Hydra-Matic transmission installed in the test car comes as standard equipment in the de Ville, Sixty Special sedan, and Eldorado convertible. The old Hydra-Matic is still being used in the Sixty-Two series and the Seventy-Five sedan and limousine. We covered the details of the Turbo Hydra-Matic pretty thoroughly in our December issue, so we won't go into that again here. We will add, though, that the torque multiplication makes the Cad a real bear off the line and that the shifts are extremely smooth and positive. We rate the new automatic right on a level with Chrysler's TorqueFlite, which we've always considered the best. (This isn't too surprising since GM's automatic is for all practical purposes identical to Chrysler's — they even pay royalties to the same inventor.) All air-conditioned cars are equipped with a 3.21 rear axle, while the others use a 2.94. The lower ratio helped acceleration in our case.

This isn't the whole performance story, though. Our test car not only had a boulevard ride that was the match of *any*, it also handled like no other big car we've ever tested. The MT crew took the test car on one extended road trip over to Phoenix, then back to Los Angeles by way of Las Vegas. During the trip, we had occasion to run on straight, smooth, high-speed freeways as well as mile after mile of up-and-

Large, plush interior sports arm rests in both front and rear seats. Grouped controls add to convenience, are balanced and pleasing. Sturdy, padded vinyl top has become de Ville hallmark.

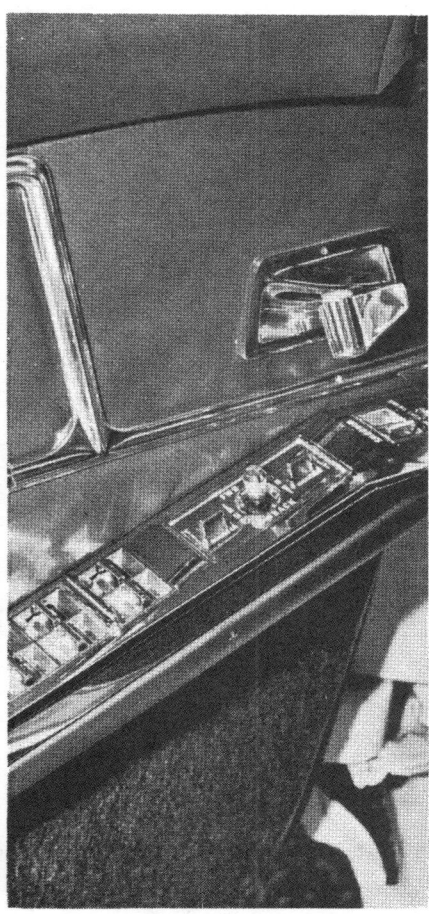

Switches for doors, windows, and seat are all grouped where driver can get at them.

Simplicity of operation of new Comfort Control air conditioner is evident here.

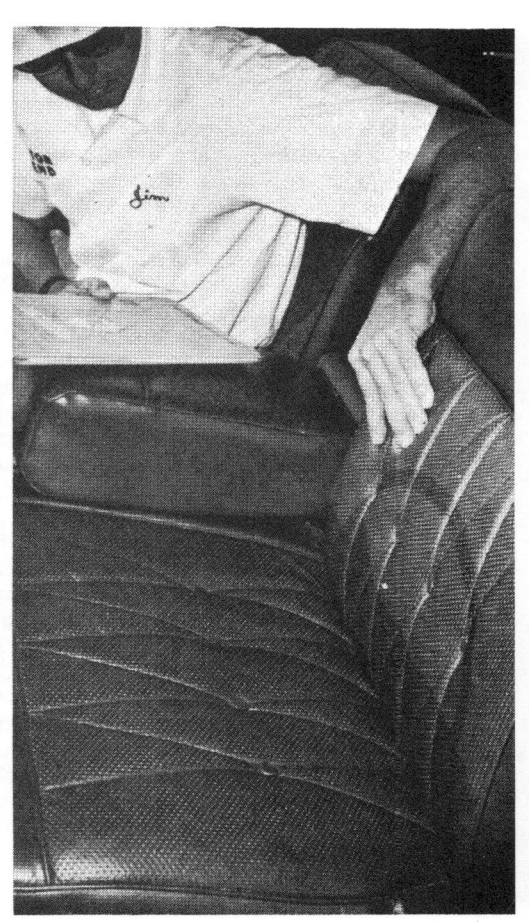

All-leather seats, optional, feature small perforations for better air circulation.

---

down, roundabout mountain roads. On the straight stretches in Nevada (where there's no speed limit), we rolled along at 110 without any concern. The big Cad is extremely stable at these high speeds, and even though some moderate crosswinds were blowing, we didn't notice them.

Over the mountain stretches, we still maintained a high average speed. We got this mostly by hard acceleration between corners, hard braking for turns, and by limit-of-adhesion cornering. We wanted to wring the car out and find its faults, if any, as well as its limitations. The faults are few (even the understeer characteristics aren't so excessive as you'd expect in a car of this size and weight — this opinion is based not only on how the car felt to us but by close inspection of the front tires after the run; they were feathered from hard cornering but weren't showing excessive wear from scrubbing), and the limitations are so far up the scale that even the worst driver will be hard-pressed to get into trouble with this car. The Cadillac may be big as a tank, but it's well balanced. Its suspension has a high degree of roll stiffness, and as the photos show, it corners very level.

The brakes held up very well during the hard use they got in the mountains. There was one stretch where we came down from 7900 feet almost to sea level — they did fade noticeably then, but we just stood on them harder and they did what was asked of them. During our test stops at Riverside, they behaved well — even survived two maximum stops from 115 mph before fading completely. The cast-iron drums

are finned and cool quickly. An added feature here is the split master cylinder that Cadillac adopted several years ago. If the front brakes go out, the rears will keep right on working — and vice versa.

We put in over 2000 miles with the test car and averaged slightly better than 13 mpg. The air conditioner was never off, and this cut mileage by 1-1½ mpg. Around town, the average was 12.5 mpg, and out on the road it was up to 14.7. This could've been better if we'd stayed around 65 mph, but we were usually up to about 75 or 85.

Much has been said about the real (and sometimes imagined) quietness of various makes of luxury cars. From past

Considering sheer size and bulk of Cadillac, handling characteristics proved outstanding. This photograph was taken on a loose, rough surface while Cad was pushing better than 70 mph.

CADILLAC SEDAN DE VILLE continued

experience, we can only say that none is quieter than our test car was. At any speed and under any condition, the air flow over and around the car was barely more than a gentle hiss. Engine and transmission noises were hardly discernible, and never did we have to turn up the radio or raise our voices because of any ambient noise.

At the risk of sounding soft, we think the most significant advance offered by Cadillac is their new air-conditioning system. This is really the unit to end all units and will no doubt be widely copied by the rest of the industry. It's called Comfort Control, and it does everything, including think for the driver. The first thing you notice is that the controls have been reduced to complete simplicity. Where there used to be as many as two or three levers *each* for both the heater and air conditioner, there are now just two. One is a control dial that incorporates temperature settings from 65° to 85° on it, and the other is a sliding lever with four settings.

Now all the driver has to do is dial the desired temperature setting, move the lever to AUTOMATIC, and forget it. From then on the system will thermostatically keep the desired temperature inside the car, regardless of outside changes. For example, we set it at 75° one morning in Phoenix and set out through the desert, where we ran into high 90° weather. Later that afternoon and evening we were in the higher regions, where the temperature dropped to 30°. The original setting hadn't been touched, yet the interior temperature was constant and completely comfortable. No more fiddling around. Theoretically, you could set it once when you buy the car and then forget about it.

The system goes on and off automatically according to demand. To do this, it uses several electronic gadgets. These include three thermistors that sense temperature changes (from outside the car, inside the car, and at the outlet of the heater/air conditioner), a potentiometer (the control dial where the driver sets the desired temperature), an amplifier, a transducer, and a power servo. A signal from any of these four sources (three thermistors and the potentiometer) is fed into the amplifier (a two-transistor unit), where it's multiplied. The amplified voltage is then fed into the transducer, which is a 10-inch steel tube with one strand of fine wire running through it. The wire is sensitive to heat, and since the amplified voltage is giving off varying amounts of heat, the wire reacts to it by either expanding or contracting slightly. This action causes a needle valve at one end of the transducer to open or close. The needle valve controls the amount of engine vacuum that will be applied to the power servo, which in turn opens or closes the air door of the heater/air conditioner. The greater the vacuum, the wider the door opens.

The servo unit also controls blower speed and at which point in the car the incoming air will be discharged. The power servo shuts off the water flow to the heater coil when maximum coolness is needed. There's another position under AUTOMATIC that gives a higher blower speed. Also controlled by the lever is the defrost action, which has a HIGH and LOW position.

As always, the Cadillac offers plenty of room on the inside — enough to allow six full-sized adults plenty of comfort on long trips. Our test car had optional leather seats — very comfortable. They were perforated with lots of tiny holes, which makes them much cooler to sit on. The six-way power seat and the adjustable steering wheel allowed us to find just the right seating position for our particular frame.

There's no need to go into any great detail about how the test car was put together. Cadillac has always had an excellent reputation for quality, and while styling and engineering might change over the years, that hasn't. /MT

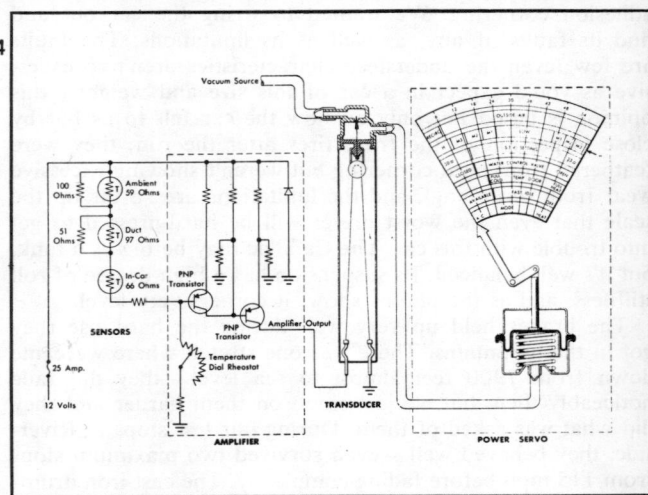

(1 THROUGH 4) New Comfort Control heater/air conditioner is probably the most important single development that this field will ever see. Theoretically, buyer can dial desired temperature when he first gets his car, then never touch it again. The unit actually has automatic controls to keep temperature constant, even though the car may be going through hot, arid deserts or low-temperature, high-altitude mountain passes. We kept constant check on both outside and inside air temperature during our extensive road test. Regardless of outside conditions, the inside was always right where we wanted it — all without touching the simple dial after its initial setting. Also shown, for you technically inclined readers, is the schematic diagram of the entire system. Complete explanation is found in text.

5) Extra inches of this year's engine plus the more efficient torque converter transmission have added quite a bit to the Cadillac's performance, combine for outstanding acceleration.

6) Stopping power proved equal to all situations. Brake fade, always present with drums, turned out to be below average — a fact attributable to the cooling fins in constant air stream.

7) Cadillac engine's basic design dates back to 1949, when it was introduced as one of the first modern, high-compression V-8s. Since then, it's been refined and enlarged somewhat.

8) No scarcity of room here. Spare location is out of the way but also a bit awkward should it have to be used. Best way to remove tire is to climb in trunk, as shown in photograph.

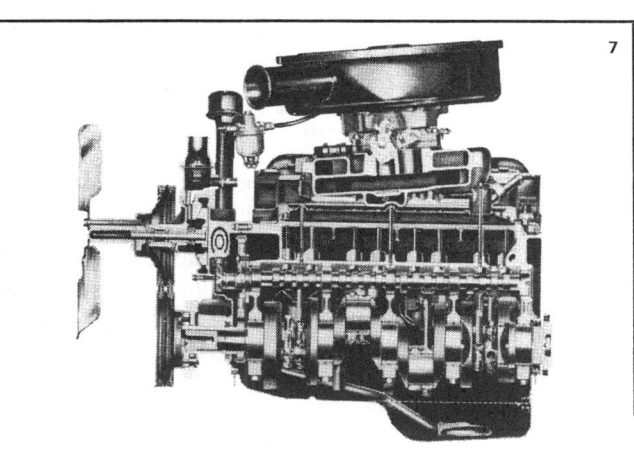

CADILLAC DE VILLE
4-door, 6-passenger sedan

OPTIONS ON CAR TESTED: Air conditioning, vinyl roof, leather seats, adjustable steering wheel, electric seat and vent windows, AM-FM radio, remote-control trunk, automatic dimmer, twilight sentinel, Cruise Control, controlled differential, rear defrost, seat belts

BASIC PRICE: $5633
PRICE AS TESTED: $7527 (plus tax and license)
ODOMETER READING AT START OF TEST: 837 miles
RECOMMENDED ENGINE RED LINE: 5200 rpm

PERFORMANCE

ACCELERATION (2 aboard)
0-30 mph............................3.4 secs.
0-45 mph............................5.7
0-60 mph............................8.5
Standing start ¼-mile 16.8 secs. and 85 mph
Speeds in gears @ 4400 rpm (shift point)
1st ....45 mph   3rd ....115 mph (actual
2nd ....80 mph   top speed)
Speedometer Error on Test Car
Car's speedometer reading 30 46 52 63 73 84
Weston electric speedometer ...30 45 50 60 70 80
Observed miles per hour per 1000 rpm in top gear ....25.5 mph
Stopping Distances — from 30 mph, 38 ft.; from 60 mph, 153 ft.

SPECIFICATIONS FROM MANUFACTURER

Engine
Ohv V-8
Bore: 4.13 ins.
Stroke: 4.0 ins.
Displacement: 429.0 cu. ins.
Compression ratio: 10.5:1
Horsepower: 340 @ 4600 rpm
Torque: 480 lbs.-ft. @ 3000 rpm
Horsepower per cubic inch: 0.79
Carburetion: 1 4-bbl.
Ignition: 12-volt coil

Gearbox
Turbo Hydra-Matic (3-speed automatic with torque converter)

Driveshaft
2-piece, open tube, with 2 constant-velocity U-joints

Differential
Hypoid, semi-floating
Standard ratio: 3.21:1

Suspension
Front: Independent, with coil springs, upper A-arm, single lower arm with strut, direct-acting tubular shocks, anti-roll bar
Rear: Rigid axle, with coil springs, 4-link stabilizer, and direct-acting tubular shocks

Steering
Ball nut sector, with integral power
Turning diameter: 43.0 ft.
Turns lock to lock: 3.7

Wheels and Tires
5-lug, steel disc wheels
8.20 x 15 4-ply nylon tubeless tires

Brakes
Hydraulic, duo-servo, self-adjusting, with split master cylinder
Front and rear: 12-in. composite cast-iron finned drums
Effective lining area: 221.8 sq. ins.

Body and Frame
Separate steel body on X-member frame
Wheelbase: 129.5 ins.
Track: front and rear, 61.0 ins.
Overall length: 223.5 ins.
Overall width: 79.7 ins.
Curb weight: 5050 lbs.

PHOTOS BY BOB D'OLIVO

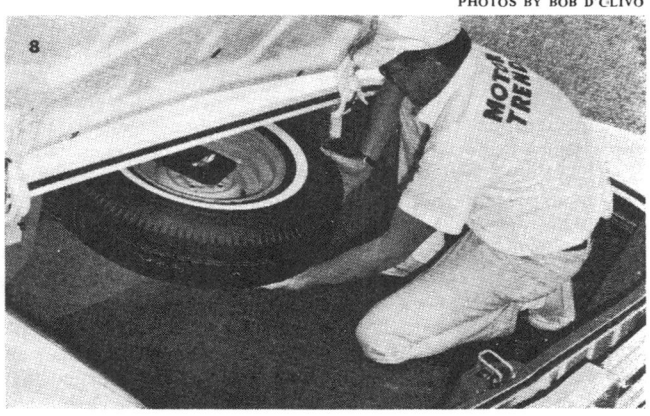

CAR LIFE ROAD TEST

CADILLAC SEDAN de VILLE

The Penalty of Leadership is Magnificently Met

IN GENERAL, people tend to view the Cadillac from one of two vantage points: Either the individual is completely attuned to this motor car or he is actively uninterested to the point of blunt skepticism. It's possible there are some who have no feelings when the name is mentioned, but the vast bulk of Americans are either like that legendary million Chevrolet owners who aspire to Cadillac ownership or are like the equally large throng that believes the car is nothing more than a vastly overrated status symbol.

Our approach to the test Cadillac Sedan de Ville was admittedly tinged with the latter outlook, from a newsjournalist's heritage of cynical objectivity. This despite the fact that the two previous Cadillacs which have undergone our scrutiny (CL, June '61 and February '63) proved thoroughly excellent vehicles. The latest test car upheld that tradition in most respects.

Cadillacs for 1964 seem little changed in appearance from the previous year, yet their styling has been refined. The now-traditional tail fins have been shaved down an inch in their inexorable march toward oblivion. The indentions separating grille and front fender have been smoothed into a massively integrated frontal aspect. Though such refinements are enough to identify the latest model, they do not significantly outdate the 1963 models. A design continuity therefore is maintained, which in turn promotes a higher resale value for "pre-owned" models.

Underneath the broad-shouldered hood, however, more than mere refinement has taken place. Cadillac had introduced a new V-8 engine for 1963, but enlarged it this year and teamed it (in the de Ville series) with a new automatic transmission. Such engineering innovations two years in a row are not exactly commonplace in the industry and bear testimony to Cadillac's determination to maintain leadership in its increasingly competitive field.

Interestingly enough, when the new engine appeared for '63 it had the same bore and stroke, and the same power rating, as the 14-year-old design it replaced. The new design, differing from the earlier in many significant ways (among which were shorter block and crankshaft length, moving all accessories except starter to the front, and a redesigned lower end), was produced for two reasons: Engine tooling had to be replaced with more modern equipment and engineers wanted a new design as a basis for future development.

As the first step in that development, the engine has been increased 10% in displacement for '64, from 390 to 429 cu. in., and the power rating boosted from 325 to 340 bhp at 4600 rpm. Bores (on 4.625-in. centers) have been widened from 4.00 in. to 4.13 in. and the stroke has been lengthened from 3.875 in. to 4.00 in. Peak torque, increased from 430 to 480 lb.-ft., is now achieved at 3000 rpm, slightly lower than before for improved city speed performance.

Pistons, though of larger diameter, are still the shorter and lighter type utilized in the '63 design and compression ratio remains at 10.5:1. A single Carter AFB carburetor with barrels of 1.438 and 1.688 in. is used. The camshaft, operating hydraulic lifters, has timing altered to 34-102-89-63° (including ramps), although the valve sizes remain at 1.875 in. intakes, 1.50 in. exhausts. Though only a single exhaust system is used, it has been increased in capacity with larger diameter piping.

The transmission in the test car (which is also used in the 60 Special sedan and Eldorado convertible of the Fleetwood series) is the GM-developed torque converter with two geared speeds and direct. Cadillac calls it the Turbo Hydra-Matic and in the near future it quite probably will (and should) be used throughout the rest of the Cadillac line still utilizing the venerable Hydra-Matic. The 3-element converter has a multiplication of 2.10:1 at stall; geared ratios are 2.48:1 first and 1.48:1 second, with Drive direct. Somewhat smoother than Hydra-Matic, the new transmission has the added advantages of providing more flexible, effective gearing, on demand, with less variation because of atmospheric pressure, and of being less complex.

With this power train, our relatively light (for Cadillac) 4-window sedan turned in some spirited—if not startling—performances. Acceleration figures show a full second is sliced off the standing ¼-mile and some 2 sec. off the 0-60 times compared with the

DOORS HAVE safety lights built into armrests, swing out wide for easy entrance.

INCREASED BORE and stroke of Cadillac V-8 gives 10% boost in displacement.

SPARE TIRE over rear axle hump leaves more room within trunk for luggage.

POWER CONSOLE is nicely arranged to give control over seats, locks, windows.

REAR DOOR armrest incorporates lighter, ash tray and window control.

CADILLAC SEDAN de VILLE

barely heavier 1963 Cadillac tested. Since shifts are made automatically at 4400 rpm (at w.o.t.), there was only a slight improvement through the forced shifts our testers used for the data panel figures. The greater torque of the engine combined with the effect of the transmission's torque multiplication launched the Cadillac off the line in truly impressive fashion, particularly when compared with earlier models and present competition.

Once at speed, the car's ride and handling proved to be a yardstick for cars in this class. It was possible to go slamming along the roughest roads with abandon, carrying the passengers along with only the mildest of nudges. One tester commented that the Cadillac had "all the feeling of a supple bridge girder."

The softness of the suspension, however, causes momentary panic during brisk cornering—until the driver accustoms himself to it. Once the car reaches full side tilt, it tenaciously plows its way around a corner; but the transition from full level to full lean is apt to be traumatic for the unwary driver.

The generous tread patch area of the huge 8.20-15 low-pressure, low-profile tires accounts for a great deal of cornering stick-to-itiveness. And the pleasantly quick power steering, though betraying only minimal road feel, is an important factor in the car's handling ease and maneuverability.

The latter attribute provided one of our most pleasant surprises about the Cadillac. Despite the car's bulk and overhanging extremities, it could easily be jockeyed about to take advantage of tight parking and turning situations, once a driver was attuned to the vehicle. The first few hours behind the wheel, however, explains why some Cadillac drivers have been accused of being road-hogs: They just don't know how much pavement the car is occupying. Once this is realized, the problem vanishes.

With the new power train well launched, Cadillac engineers might turn their attention to the brakes. The 377 sq. in. of swept lining area would seem to be none too generous, since even in our relatively light test car they faded completely during our all-on stops from 80 mph. Deceleration rates were hardly spectacular, at 20 and 18 ft./sec./sec., and even around town their effectiveness seemed hardly in keeping with the car's character.

Character the Cadillac does have—in vast amounts. From the optional vinyl-covered roof to the nostalgic fender skirts at the rear wheel openings, the car can be summed up in one word: Polish. What other automobile can boast of hard gold contact points in its voltage regulator?

The momentary confusion of a first glance at the control panel (it hardly can be called an instrument panel any longer) quickly gives way to admiration for the logical layout. Our testers, at least, found that all controls are well-placed at the exact location where one unconsciously reaches for them. Only the trip odometer reset knob evaded us for awhile, but later was discovered hiding 'way back under the lower lip of the dashboard.

The cruise control, which was the most consistent and responsive of all such devices we've tried so far, was conveniently spotted on the dashboard to the left of the wheel. Once locked on, it was possible to fly the freeways by merely rolling on or off a notch or so of speed trim (providing the traffic wasn't too heavy). A similar control, rolling horizontally, operates the electronic thermostat for the combined heater/air conditioner "Comfort Control." This device had a tendency to be somewhat noisy, but then that probably was because of the high degree of sound deadening and silence engineered into the rest of the car.

Another item which added to the fun and games when driving the Cadillac was the "Twilight Sentinel," an automatic headlight switch operated by a photocell in the lip of the dashboard hood. This switched on the lights at dusk (or when driving into a garage) and then turned them off automatically —after a variable interval of up to 90 sec.—once the key was turned off. A conventional headlight switch is also fitted for those who find it difficult to accept such automation. There were many other items over which to exclaim: But most of all, there was the pure sensual pleasure of turning the key, setting the speed and climate dials to 70, and settling back to effortlessly guide the Cadillac into the gathering dusk with only the squeak of the perforated leather cushions, as you move to a comfortable position, to annoy you. With all that power-assisted automation, Cadillac probably needed the larger engine as much to drive the accessories as to be powered somewhere near its competitors.

There is an old and very famous Cadillac advertisement which had, as an opening line, "The Penalty of Leadership . . ." And no other statement could better sum up our own impressions of the 1964 Cadillac. Being a leader presents problems, invites hypercritical examination and encourages adverse comments. Yet our test crew, after 10 days with the new Cadillac, came away marveling at the magnificent manner in which that "penalty" is being paid. ∎

CAR LIFE ROAD TEST

1964 CADILLAC
Sedan de Ville Hardtop

SPECIFICATIONS
List price	$5655
Price, as tested	6932
Curb weight, lb	4900
Test weight	5230
distribution, %	53/47
Tire size	8.20-15
Tire capacity, lb	5660
Brake swept area	377
Engine type	V-8, ohv
Bore & stroke	4.13 x 4.00
Displacement, cu. in	429
Compression ratio	10.5
Carburetion	1 x 4
Bhp @ rpm	340 @ 4600
equivalent mph	120
Torque, lb-ft	480 @ 3000
equivalent mph	77.8

DIMENSIONS
Wheelbase, in	129.5
Tread, f & r	61.0
Overall length, in	223.5
width	79.7
height	54.8
equivalent vol, cu. ft	581
Frontal area, sq. ft	25.0
Ground clearance, in	5.28
Steering ratio, o/a	18.2
turns, lock to lock	3.7
turning circle, ft	43.0
Hip room, front	63.4
Hip room, rear	63.6
Pedal to seat back, max	43.0
Floor to ground	13.0
Luggage vol, cu. ft	15.8
Fuel tank capacity, gal	26

EXTRA-COST OPTIONS
Leather upholstery, vinyl roof cover, power windows, Twilight Sentinel, comfort control, cruise control, tinted glass, AM/FM radio, tilting wheel.

GEAR RATIOS
3rd (1.00) overall	3.21
2nd (1.48)	4.75
1st (2.48)	7.96
1st (2.10 x 2.48)	16.7

CALCULATED DATA
Lb/bhp (test wt)	15.1
Cu. ft/ton mile	112
Mph/1000 rpm	26.0
Engine revs/mile	2310
Piston travel, ft/mile	1540
Car Life wear index	35.6

SPEEDOMETER ERROR
30 mph, actual	29.8
60 mph	57.0
90 mph	86.5

FUEL CONSUMPTION
Normal range, mpg	9-12

PERFORMANCE
Top speed (4650), mph	121
Shifts,@ mph (auto., forced)	
3rd ( )	
2nd (4400)	77
1st (4400)	46
Total drag at 60 mph, lb	160

ACCELERATION
0-30 mph, sec.	3.4
0-40	4.8
0-50	6.5
0-60	8.5
0-70	11.0
0-80	14.1
0-100	23.5
Standing ¼ mile, sec.	16.4
speed at end, mph	86

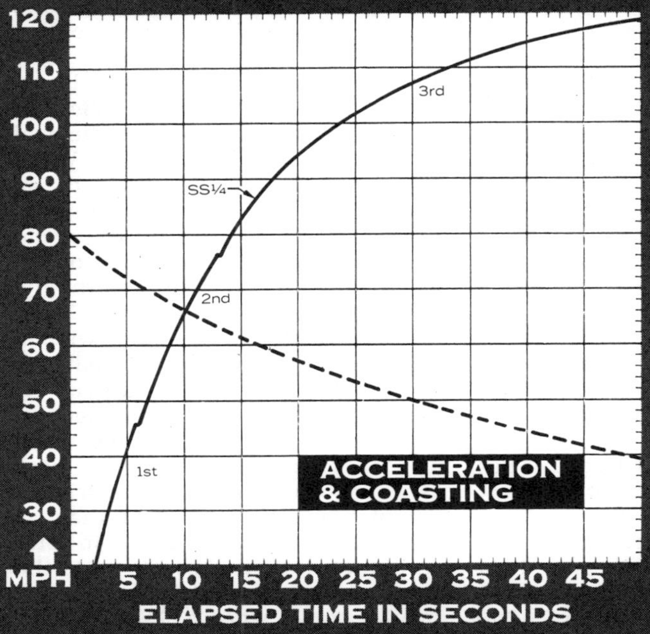

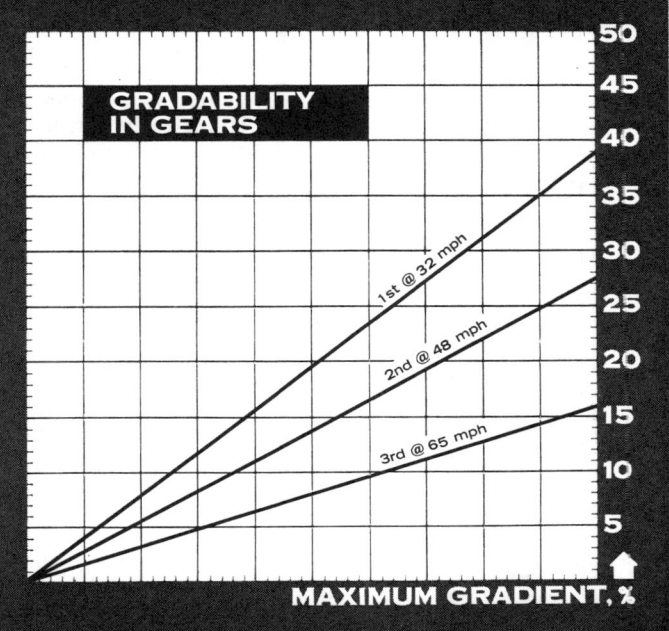

THE 1965s ARE HERE!

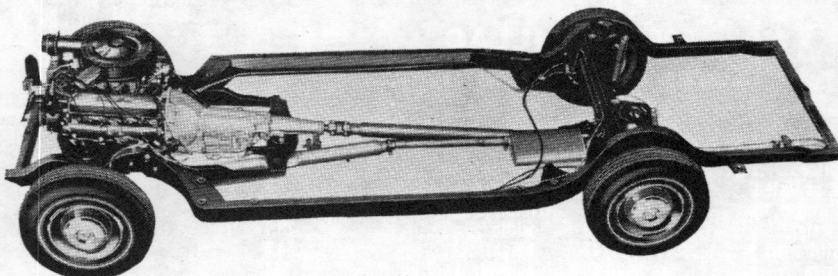

CADILLAC: When the 1961 Lincoln Continental appeared, Cadillac stylists were already thinking about a graceful way to get rid of the tail fins. But the success of the Lincoln convinced them that simplicity in overall design was even more important. The result is a completely restyled 1965 Cadillac of very sensible proportions, a total absence of styling gimmicks, and a general appearance obviously related to the Oldsmobile 98 and the Buick Electra 225, yet clearly distinguishable as a Cadillac.

In Cadillac's most dramatic styling and engineering change in post-war years, suspension and frame design is basically similar to the new Buick and Oldsmobile chassis, with a perimeter frame allowing the engine to be moved six inches forward and the floor tunnel to be appreciably lowered. Both front and rear track are increased 1½ inches, and a new four-arm linkage is used to locate the rear axle.

The new Turbo Hydra-Matic transmission is standard, and the engine remains unchanged from 1964—a quietly efficient lightweight 340-bhp 429-cu.in. V-8.

It's well known that Cadillac has an experimental V-12 power unit just about ready, but it's not common knowledge that they came very close to producing it for the 1965 models. We are sorry they didn't because it would have given Cadillac an exclusivity of outstanding merit and raised the prestige of the marque well above that of its competition (Continental and Imperial, as well as served to emphasize the supremacy and independence of Cadillac's engineering department within the dictates of General Motors Corporation.

In the interior, all the usual luxury options continue, starting with power windows and door locks, six-way power seats, tilt-and-telescope steering wheel, Cruise Control, automatic headlight dimmer and ending up with the Harrison/Frigidaire Climate Control. A new option (standard on the Eldorado convertible) consists of an automatic leveling device which maintains the rear end at normal height regardless of passenger or luggage loads. When there's a change in the load, an individual engine-driven compressor adjusts the setting of two special shock absorbers, and the tail of the car is raised or lowered accordingly.

We stopped thinking about Cadillacs as terrestrial battleships when a Series 62 in stock trim finished 10th overall in the 24-hour race at Le Mans in 1950, but the engineering improvements for 1965 have made us look at the Cadillac even more as a car for our next trip to Bridgehampton or Watkins Glen than as a vehicle of which we'll live in total ignorance until we have to go to the opera one night, or to a funeral, or the day comes when a GM executive offers us a ride from the airport.

CAR and DRIVER/JULY 1965

PHOTOGRAPHY: TOM BURNSIDE

SIX LUXURY CARS

A subjective, seat-of-the-pants evaluation by the editors

There are more myths about luxury cars than any other automobile category that comes to mind. How many otherwise well-informed citizens do you know who believe steadfastly that the Rolls-Royce engine compartment is sealed at the factory, or that all Rolls-Royces enjoy a lifetime warranty?

Among purists, there are some other myths as well. Like, "All American cars are lousy, and the Cadillac is just a chromed-up Chevrolet." It's strange, but the anti-American-car syndrome, so prevalent with the tweed-cap crowd, also seems to rub off a bit on German cars. When we first announced and described the then-new Mercedes-Benz 600, we got dozens of letters, alternately dripping with sarcasm or invective, loftily pointing out that there was simply no way that the Germans could build a car to compete equally with England's and God's own Rolls-Royce.

We decided to test six luxury cars against each other to prove or disprove some of the old adages. The evaluation is broken down into three parts—this subjective look at the six as a prospective buyer might see them; a detailed technical examination by Eric Nielssen, on page **64**, con-

SIX LUXURY CARS

siderably more objective in tone; and a comparative checklist on page 67, rating the cars competitively on a one-to-ten point basis. This involved borrowing a series of different cars of each make for weekend trips and normal day-to-day use over a period of about six months. We then arranged to have all six simultaneously for a comparative evaluation, which took place on the South Shore of Long Island at one of the huge paved parking fields for the public beaches there.

In all of our driving and comparing, we tried to think of the cars and their performance from the standpoint of the American driver who'd need, want, or buy such a conveyance. Being enthusiasts, we could not filter out enthusiast considerations completely, but we tried to stay within the parameters of luxury and quality in the bulk of our evaluations. We were most interested in interior comfort, silence, quality of materials, function and convenience of accessories and optional equipment, ride, and driving ease—these being, in our minds, prime considerations in the selection of a luxury car.

The luxury car buyer wants and deserves an automobile that does its job without bugging him. He wants it to look good, feel good, run well, last a long time, and do it all without any fuss—without requiring more than minimal attention from him, either as owner or driver. A luxury car should offer anything and everything its driver requires for maximum comfort and pleasure, and it was on this basis that we judged the relative merits of our six contenders for the luxury crown.

It's amazing how quickly quality and performance differences will show up in similar cars when they can be directly compared, *en bloc,* as it were, as we did these six luxury cars. Flaws and faults became immediately apparent, and it was easy to make the necessary qualitative judgements. Any one of the cars, away from the rest, is apt to seem like a pretty decent machine. But with the six thrown together, competing feature for feature, some important differences came to light.

The Mercedes-Benz 600 was the hands-down winner—utterly beyond the reach of the others. The Cadillac was a strong and undisputed second, perhaps the biggest surprise of the whole test project. The Lincoln Continental was third by a narrow margin over the Rolls-Royce, which in turn barely edged out the Imperial. Jaguar's 4.2 Sedan (Mark X) was sixth, not so much because it was in any way inferior to the rest as an *automobile,* but because it simply isn't the same kind of car that they are. It's smaller, considerably less posh, and has obviously been aimed more at the sporting driver. It's a luxurious sports sedan, but it is *not* a luxury car. Since Jaguar has chosen to market it as a luxury car, and since we had already included it in the testing program, we elected to leave it in, but the reader should mentally hold it off to one side, in a category of its own.

So let's compare . . .

The Mercedes-Benz 600 The Mercedes-Benz 600 proved to our complete satisfaction, that it is the best car in the world. A top executive at Cadillac paid it a light-hearted compliment when he said, "It's probably the ultimate Cadillac," and in many ways, he was dead right. The Mercedes is a *complete* luxury car, and it is far more American in concept than any previous European effort in this field. It has, and will do, virtually everything one could ask of it. Its performance is superior to any other car in its class. Only the Cadillac can out-accelerate it. Only the Jaguar can go around a corner with it. Only the Rolls was able to approach its enormous stopping power.

The Mercedes would possibly have been able to win our six-way competition on the strength of its luxury alone, but it has married that luxury to a mechanical package of tremendous sophistication in the grand Mercedes tradition. Imagine if you can, a car with every luxury appointment known, a car that Stirling Moss can load with six full-grown adults and hurl around Brands Hatch within five seconds of the lap record for sedans, and you'll be getting an idea of what we mean.

62

All power assists and controls are hydraulic, so they operate in absolute silence—even the windshield wipers sweep back and forth across the glass without a sound. Both front and rear seats are adjustable, as are the shock absorbers. The trunk lid opens and closes with hydraulic silence, like a secret panel in a horror film (it is unfortunately true that it opens to expose a ridiculously small trunk but perhaps they expect us to carry only our immediate personal needs in the car, leaving the rest for a servant to bring in a 220-SE, or something).

Some things annoyed us about the 600. Its automatic transmission has sacrificed smoothness for maximum mechanical efficiency, which results in very stiff shifts (but is probably a major factor in the car's amazing acceleration, in spite of its unspectacular power-to-weight ratio). The instruments and controls have been lifted intact from the rest of the (lower-priced) Mercedes line, and this seems unworthy of a $20,000 automobile. Many of the small controls are poorly marked—in fact, the first-time driver isn't given a *clue* about wipers, headlights, shock absorber adjustment, heater-defroster-air conditioner, or a number of other mysterious little switches that activate one-knows-not-what. The quadrant for the automatic transmission selector is clear over to the left, tucked away in the lower half of the tachometer dial, where *nobody* finds it without a diligent search of the instrument panel. And finally, the front seat ashtrays are incorporated in the armrest-doorpull-window-lift unit in such a way that a smoking driver is forced to look at the ashtray—which is also too small—in order to flick the ash from a cigarette or cigar while driving.

As you can see, these flaws aren't critical, being more aptly described as minor annoyances, but they do mar the near-perfection of an otherwise superior automobile.

The Mercedes-Benz 600—like the Rolls-Royce—hews to a tradition. But where Rolls-Royce slavishly pursues an almost baroque dedication to form, as opposed to function, the Mercedes tradition is all function. The car was designed—not styled—to carry five adults in tastefully elegant, supremely comfortable splendor at speeds up to 128 mph, with handling and stability and brakes that should arouse envy in most sports cars—a noble purpose, and one that Daimler-Benz has achieved with almost unqualified success.

From the outside, it makes no bones about what it is. It is a rectangular box, its flat sides and square corners compromised only where it was necessary to incorporate wheels and engine and luggage space. The rather ponderous use of chrome only seems to underline this fact—not Freudian, not the result of misapplied motivational research, just an engineer's notion of where some bright metal highlights were needed, topped, as always, by the Silver Star. The effect of all this pugnacious-looking self-confidence is a bit awe-inspiring—like watching Babe Ruth point to the spot where he was going to poke his next home run and *knowing*, just sure as hell, that he could do it.

This Mercedes will do it too, just sure as hell.

The Cadillac Fleetwood Brougham Among enthusiasts, the Cadillac is probably the most underrated car in the world, although in some ways, it equals or excels the Mercedes 600. It is certainly the best bargain of the whole lot of luxury cars, if words like bargain and luxury can be used in the same sentence. It has more useful features than the rest, particularly for comfort and convenience. For instance, the steering wheel has ample, easy adjustment for both reach and rake, and with the wide range of adjustment possible in the six-way power seat, it's hard to imagine anyone who couldn't find a completely comfortable driving position. Unlike the Mercedes' seats, where you sit more-or-less where you were put, the Cadillac's are comfortable in almost any position, from bolt upright to upside down like a teenage moppet on the phone.

And, there's the steering wheel itself, which is small in diameter with an almost-dainty rim-thickness. Why all cars equipped with power steering don't use a similar wheel is a mystery—the Mercedes, for instance, has no steering wheel adjustment of any kind, and although the power steering

(Text continued on page 70; technical analysis overleaf)

"It's amazing how quickly quality and performance differences show up when cars can be directly compared. ..."

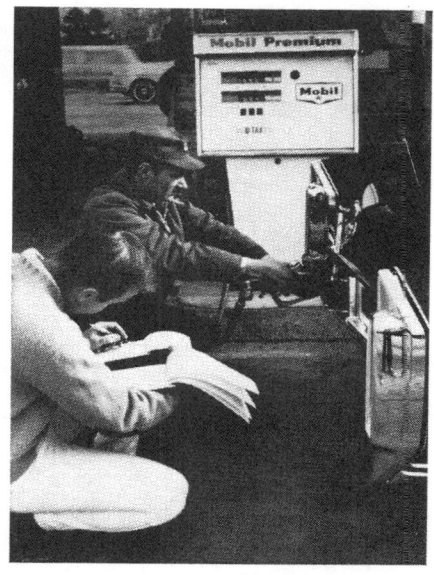

SIX LUXURY CARS: a view from

Cadillac Fleetwood Brougham, $8,359.55

Lincoln Continental, $7,472.45

The most notable technical characteristics our six luxury cars have in common is their almost unrelieved orthodoxy. At the opposite, "mini-car", end of the scale there is rampant heterodoxy and frequent disagreement up the range, but these Big Ones, the carriages for the carriage trade, have never in their history experienced a significant deviation from the front-engine, rear-drive formula.

Take suspension for example. These cars demand the ultimate in ride comfort, but with laden weights ranging from 4650 to 5780 pounds, exotic suspensions are not essential to the achievement of high sprung/unsprung weight ratios. Thus, only two of the six have independent rear suspension, and only one makes use of air suspension. All have wishbones in front, the Imperial retaining torsion bar springs, and three have leaf springs in back. Cadillac and Jaguar have coils all around.

Front wheel suspension rates range from a low of 86 pounds per inch for Cadillac, to a high of 120 for the Lincoln, the point being that this is not much variation. There's even less at the rear, from 110 for Cadillac and Lincoln, to 125 for Imperial. The Mercedes, due to its pressurized rubber bags, was not included in this rate comparison. It's been made adaptable to different road and load conditions by a two-position adjustable shock absorber system. The 600 suspension is inherently of a much lower rate than the others, and for stable operation at the high speeds of which the car is capable it requires fairly heavy damping. This is usually compromised with the need for a "boulevard ride", but Daimler-Benz engineers were willing to make no compromise: hence the two-position shockers. Rolls-Royce has a similar provision for the rear wheels only, and Cadillac has a compressed-air vehicle leveling system for the back end which raises the rear spring rate to restore normal trim when the car is laden.

Only in the Jaguar was handling, in terms of maximum cornering power, ranked as a design objective equal to or above sheer ride comfort. Only the Mark X (sorry, Jaguar, but I can't get used to "4.2 Sedan") was willing to take on the high-frequency sound transmission problems presented by radial-cord tire construction (Dunlop SP41, to be precise). Wheel size is 14 inches with an approximate 7.50 tire section. All the others run on 15-inch

the Automotive Engineering Side

wheels with tire sections of 9.00 or 9.15 except Cadillac which has an 8.00 section as standard.

Power steering has long been standard on cars of this class which perhaps accounts for their uniformly quick steering ratios. All but the Rolls need less than four turns lock to lock; all but the Jaguar have poor turning circles, closer to 50 feet in diameter than 40. The Mark X combines a 38-foot circle with a mere three turns lock to lock, achieved with a new Bishop patent Merles Varamatic Bendix steering gear, which provides a significant variable-ratio feature. Near center position, where you need sensitive control, the ratio is equivalent to 4.25 turns, and as you turn to each side it rapidly and progressively "speeds up" to the equivalent of 2.1 turns, to make parking maneuvers quick as well as easy. All six cars use belts to drive the hydraulic pump except Lincoln, which mounts it directly on the nose of the crankshaft.

On the question of separate frames versus integral construction, this half-dozen is divided right down the middle. Those with separate frames are Rolls-Royce, Imperial and Cadillac. The Rolls frame is a lofty and classic design, with box-section side members seven inches high and 3½ inches wide and a cruciform center brace that keeps the floorboards and passengers well clear of the drive shaft and the ground. The torsional stiffness of the Rolls frame alone is rated at 2700 pound-feet per degree of twist.

Lower but similar in broad principle is the box frame of the Imperial, with normal crossmembers in the closed models and a cruciform center section in the convertibles, both being the only separate-frame models made in the U.S. by Chrysler. Cadillac in 1965 made its first major frame change in nine years, from a pure perimeter layout. Considerable added strength both in beam and torsion is derived from its Fisher body.

The other three cars can be said to have platform-integral frames—there's no separate frame, but most of the strength is in the lower part of the body, the sills and the floor or "platform". Jaguar, in fact, says that the Mark X would lose nothing in stiffness if the roof and pillars were sawed off (which may give you ideas). The strength is concentrated in the very high and wide body sills which tend to make entry more dif-

Mercedes-Benz 600, $20,500.00

Rolls-Royce Silver Cloud III, $17,321.00

Jaguar Mark X, 4.2 liter, $6,990.00

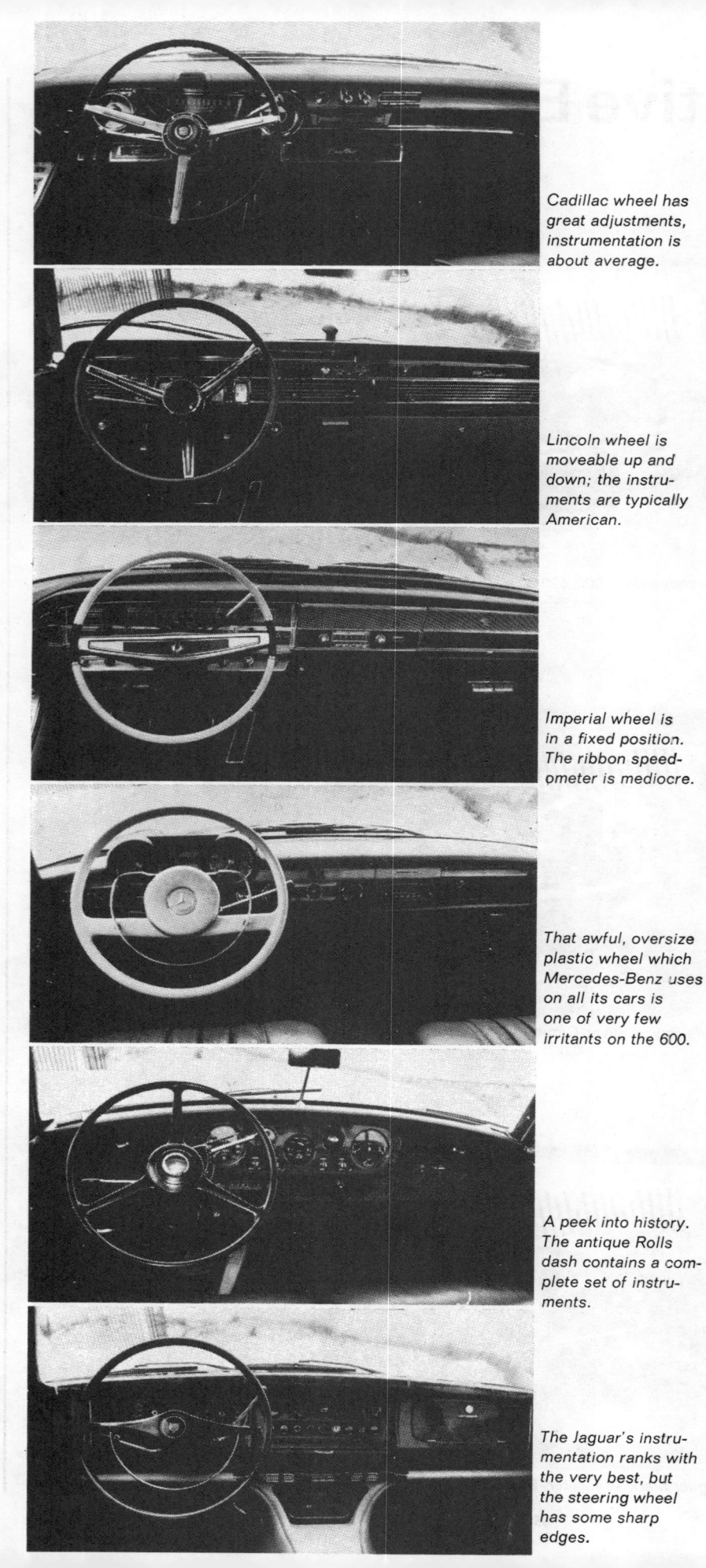

Cadillac wheel has great adjustments, instrumentation is about average.

Lincoln wheel is moveable up and down; the instruments are typically American.

Imperial wheel is in a fixed position. The ribbon speedometer is mediocre.

That awful, oversize plastic wheel which Mercedes-Benz uses on all its cars is one of very few irritants on the 600.

A peek into history. The antique Rolls dash contains a complete set of instruments.

The Jaguar's instrumentation ranks with the very best, but the steering wheel has some sharp edges.

ficult than is usual in this class of car.

The Jaguar design was introduced in October 1961. Just a year earlier Lincoln brought out a new platform-integral design, a structure two-thirds stiffer torsionally than its integral predecessor. This rated it at over 10,000 pound-feet per degree, a very high torsional stiffness for American sedans. When Mercedes brought out the 600 in September 1963, they had also chosen the platform frame. Acutely conscious of the need for very high stiffness to increase the natural frequencies of the vehicle for maximum silence in running, they came up with a platform/body combination that is five times stiffer than the Mercedes-Benz Grand Prix car of 1955, making it well in excess of 15,000 pound-feet per degree. They did it, in part, by making the prop-shaft tunnel a torsionally stiff backbone and by using an analog computer to work out the best sheet metal thicknesses for weight and strength. The 600 frame alone was as stiff as the combined frame and body of its forerunner, the 300D.

All of these automobiles are fast (115+ mph) as well as heavy, posing special problems in the brake department. On all of them power boost is standard: the three Americans and the Jaguar having vacuum assistance, the Rolls its remarkable mechanical servo, and the German a compressed air system using the suspension air supply. The most conventional brakes are the Imperial's, with 11-inch drums all around. Cadillac has 12-inch finned iron drums, applied by a dual-circuit master cylinder; and Rolls-Royce has 11.25-inch drums with two trailing-shoe mechanisms for maximum fade resistance.

After a transition period with aluminum front drums, Lincoln changed over to Kelsey-Hayes ventilated 11.87-inch disc brakes in front in 1965. A pressure-limiting valve in the hydraulic system delays lockup of the 11.09-inch rear drum brakes. The Mercedes-Benz 600 has discs at all wheels, 11.25-inch in front and 11.6-inch in the rear. The heavier braking loads at the front wheels are taken by thicker discs and by the unusual use of two separate calipers at each wheel. Each of the front brakes is able to dissipate energy at a rate of 450 horsepower, each of the rears at 250 horsepower. That gives the Mercedes 1400 horses of stopping power which is not excessive if you consider that the maximum allowable weight of the 153.5-inch-wheelbase version is 7320 pounds.

Jaguar, European pioneer of production four-wheel discs, retains Dunlop calipers on the Mark X. The discs are not large compared to the others we've looked at (10.9 inches in diameter in front and 10.4 inches in the back). Sizes are limited respectively by the 14-inch wheels and the inboard mounting of the rear brakes, next to the differential.

In the engine room, as in other departments, the Jaguar does not lend itself to an across-the-board comparison with the other five. This is quite understandable. All the others are luxury cars by birthright, as well as by design. They've been moving in the top circles for decades. Though Jaguars no longer deserve to be slighted as "the Bentleys of Wardour Street", they would be the first to admit that their product has been steadily extended from Marks VII and VIII through IX to keep pace with the luxury leaders. This is particularly true of the engine which they reluctantly expanded to 231 cubic inches and now, by enlarged dry liners, have further bored to 258 cubes to keep pace with the quick Americans. The twin-cam six has to turn to 5400 rpm to develop its 265 horsepower, which is too fast for too little.

The Jaguar and the Imperial are the only cars in the group that share their engines with lesser vehicles. This shows refreshing individuality in these days of interchangeability. All but the Jaguar are oversquare V-8s, cast iron except for the Rolls block and heads and the Mercedes heads (aluminum, like the Mark X head). The Americans range from 413 to 430 cubic inches, and develop peak power at 4600 rpm. Peak torques are massive, from 465 (Lincoln) to 480 pound-feet (Cadillac), developed at an average of 2800 rpm.

Somewhat surprisingly, the two European V-8s are both smaller and slower with 380+ cubic inches and 4100 rpm peaking speeds. As Rolls-Royce says, "We do not sell rpm, because they are always audible. If you try to run an engine faster to get more performance, you have to mask the fuss you have created." The Rolls V-8, announced in September 1959, probably develops the same 300 horsepower (gross) delivered by the Mercedes engine which is exactly four years newer. Torque of both is in the 430+ pound-feet area. Jaguar, by contrast, can offer only 283 pound-feet at a relatively-high 4000 rpm. In view of this comparison it's not surprising that the Coventry firm is rumored to have both a V-8 and a V-12 in the works.

Cadillac, with the highest compression of the group (10.5 to one),

CHECK LIST (Cars rated numerically, with 10 as maximum)	Mercedes-Benz 600	Cadillac Brougham	Lincoln Continental	Rolls-Royce Silver Cloud III	Imperial LeBaron	Jaguar 4.2 Liter
ENGINE						
Starting	8	10	10	10	10	9
Response	10	8	4	5	4	4
Noise	8	10	7	10	7	2
Vibration	9	10	7	10	8	7
DRIVE TRAIN						
Transmission controls	5	9	9	2	8	7
Shift smoothness	5	10	7	3	8	3
BRAKES						
Response	10	6	7	10	6	7
Pedal pressure	8	7	7	9	7	6
Fade resistance	10	5	7	9	4	10
Smoothness	10	7	7	10	5	9
Directional stability	5	5	8	10	2	8
STEERING						
Response	10	6	5	6	5	7
Accuracy	10	7	6	5	6	9
Feedback	10	5	5	5	4	9
Road feel	10	6	6	7	6	10
SUSPENSION						
Harshness control	7	10	8	3	5	3
Roll stiffness	10	8	7	3	6	9
Tracking	10	9	6	4	4	9
Pitch control	9	9	7	5	7	5
Shock damping	10	5	6	6	6	6
CONTROLS						
Location	10	9	8	5	9	5
Relationship	10	9	8	7	8	6
Small controls	5	9	4	5	6	5
INTERIOR						
Visibility	10	7	7	5	7	7
Instrumentation	9	5	5	6	5	9
Lighting	10	6	5	5	6	4
Entry/exit	9	9	9	3	5	4
Storage space	10	2	5	5	5	3
Wind noise	8	9	9	7	7	5
Road noise	8	9	8	7	4	6
WEATHER PROTECTION						
Ventilation	10	5	5	6	4	3
Weather sealing	10	9	5	10	5	6
Windshield wiper action	6	6	7	3	4	5
Heater/defroster/air conditioner	9	10	7	6	7	1
QUALITY CONTROL						
Materials, exterior	10	8	4	10	4	6
Materials, interior	10	9	5	10	2	7
Exterior finish	10	8	3	10	3	4
Interior finish	10	9	4	10	5	5
Hardware and trim	10	8	4	10	5	6
GENERAL						
Service accessibility	8	7	7	5	6	5
Bumper protection	6	9	9	7	7	5
Exterior lighting	8	10	9	5	8	7
Resistance to crosswinds	9	9	8	9	7	7
Luggage space	5	10	9	5	10	6
COMFORT (based on 5-passenger load, 2 front, 3 rear)						
Steering wheel position	5	10	7	4	4	7
Shoulder room, front	9	9	8	5	9	5
Shoulder room, rear	8	8	8	5	8	5
Hip room, front	9	8	8	5	9	4
Hip room, rear	8	8	8	5	8	4
Leg room, front	9	9	9	7	9	7
Leg room, rear	8	8	6	6	8	5
Head room	8	7	7	6	8	6
Seat adjustment	9	9	7	5	7	5
Seat design	9	8	6	7	6	4
TOTAL	466	427	364	348	333	319
AVERAGE SCORE	8.6	7.9	6.7	6.4	6.2	5.9

Sets of men's and women's luggage were provided for test by American Tourister.

Only the Cadillac (left) and the Imperial (right) accommodated all of the luggage.

The 600's trunk (left) was among the smallest, but the Lincoln took all but one bag.

Both the Rolls-Royce (left) and the Jaguar Mark X had rather limited luggage space.

is also the lightest per horsepower with an engine weight of 600 pounds. Jaguar is next, at about 625 pounds, followed by Imperial, Rolls-Royce and Lincoln at 675, 713 and 735 pounds respectively. The Mercedes V-8, whose weight has not been disclosed, is likely the heaviest of the lot with its single overhead camshaft on each bank and its timed Bosch fuel injection system. Unlike the Jaguar, the overhead cams of the Mercedes have not been exploited to gain a power advantage, so their presence must be ascribed to (a) tradition and (b) possible future development as power for a Corvette-chasing 600SL sports car.

The last Cadillac on which a manual transmission was offered was the Series 75 chassis of 1953. Automatics were on all standard Cadillacs and Lincolns that year, have been ever since, and are still the only transmissions available on our sample six. (You can get a Mark X with a four-speed floor shift, but not in this country.)

Rolls-Royce continues to manufacture its own version of the old four-speed Hydra-Matic under General Motors license. Like GM over the years, Rolls has worked hard to smooth out the inherently firm shifts of the Hydra-Matic without ruining fuel consumption in the process. Now that GM has shifted entirely to the three-speed box plus torque converter with an inherently smoother gear change (see the Cadillac Turbo Hydra-Matic, and the similar and earlier Lincoln Turbo-Drive and Imperial Torque Flite), it's interesting to speculate that Rolls-Royce may be thinking of making a similar transition.

Like so many European manufacturers today, Jaguar buys its automatics from Borg-Warner. This again is a torque converter plus three-speed planetary box. Daimler-Benz, on the other hand, decided to design its own automatic box with hydraulic coupling and four forward speeds, in broad principle like the Hydra-Matic, but entirely different in actual design.

On luxury automobiles the drive line is regarded as a source of noise as well as an intrusion on footroom, and usually receives special attention. One-piece drive shafts are used by Lincoln and Cadillac. Lincoln damps out vibration by making the shaft of two concentric tubes joined by eight rubber "torque rings", which transmit the drive in shear. Lincoln uses a constant-velocity universal joint at the front end, and Cadillac uses them at both ends of the shaft.

Two-piece shafts with central

steady bearings are found on the rest, and Mercedes-Benz and Imperial also use constant-velocity joints to smooth out power transmission. Jaguar's frame-mounted final drive unit, a potential source of harshness in the drive, has been rubber-mounted to allow a 5° rotation under traction and a 3° rotation under braking, thus providing a cushioning effect. Only Jaguar and Mercedes offer limited-slip differentials as standard equipment.

Much of the technical story of these cars lies in the remarkable range of options and accessories available, from the automatic speed control of the Americans to the self-latching doors of the Mercedes 600. Not so often described is the problem of providing power for all the energy-consuming devices, i.e., this list for a four-door Imperial:

Four window lift motors, two vent window motors, windshield wiper motor, windshield washer motor, radio, radio antenna motor, heater motor, rear seat defroster motor, two seat adjusting motors, four door-locking solenoids, three cigar lighters, four headlamps and approximately thirty-three other lamps throughout the instrument panel and the rest of the body.

Rolls-Royce fits a 35-amp generator to meet such demands. Cadillac and Lincoln have 42 amps as standard (55 with air conditioning). Mercedes estimates the maximum requirement to be 45 amps and meets it with two separate Bosch alternators producing a total of 70 amps. They're driven at slightly different speeds so that one of them can be more effective at idle.

Mercedes actually shoulders most of its accessory load with a unique high-pressure hydraulic system, allowing actuating cylinders which weigh substantially less than equivalent electric motors. Since it is required to do only light duty, it is pressurized at only one-tenth the 3000 psi used in the Citroën DS-19, which uses hydraulics to hold up the car, apply the brakes, etc. The small and silent fluid lines on the Mercedes 600 are used to raise and lower windows, adjust the seats, shock absorbers and sliding roof, open and latch the trunk lid and doors, release the hand-brake, and adjust the valves in the heating/cooling system. No such light-duty systems existed in economical form, so Daimler-Benz had to develop its own ways to manufacture the little double-acting hydraulic cylinders and attach the required piping reliably and easily. *(Continued on page 72)*

MERCEDES-BENZ 600

Price as tested:	$20,500
Length	218 in.
Height	59.5 in.
Width	76.8 in.
Curb weight	5380 lbs.
Wheelbase	126 in.
Engine type	DOHC V-8
Displacement	386 cu. in.
Horsepower	300 bhp @ 4100 rpm
Torque	434 lb-ft @ 3000 rpm
Carburetion	Bosch injection
Transmission	4-speed automatic

Acceleration:
- 0–30 mph ... 3.2 sec.
- 0–40 mph ... 4.9 sec.
- 0–50 mph ... 7.0 sec.
- 0–60 mph ... 9.4 sec.
- 0–70 mph ... 12.3 sec.
- 0–80 mph ... 16.5 sec.

Mileage ... 10.91 mpg
80 mph to rest: panic stop ... 4.7 sec.

LINCOLN CONTINENTAL

Price as tested:	$7,472.45
Length	216.5 in.
Height	54.5 in.
Width	78.5 in.
Curb weight	5280 lbs.
Wheelbase	126 in.
Engine type	OHV V-8
Displacement	430 cu. in.
Horsepower	320 bhp @ 4600 rpm
Torque	465 lb-ft @ 2600 rpm
Carburetion	1 Holley 4-bbl
Transmission	3-speed automatic

Acceleration:
- 0–30 mph ... 3.7 sec.
- 0–40 mph ... 5.6 sec.
- 0–50 mph ... 8.0 sec.
- 0–60 mph ... 11.3 sec.
- 0–70 mph ... 15.1 sec.
- 0–80 mph ... 19.4 sec.

Mileage ... 13.26 mpg
80 mph to rest: panic stop ... 5.3 sec.

IMPERIAL LE BARON

Price as tested:	$5,596.43
Length	228 in.
Height	57 in.
Width	80 in.
Curb weight	5035 lbs.
Wheelbase	129 in.
Engine type	OHV V-8
Displacement	413 cu. in.
Horsepower	340 bhp @ 4600 rpm
Torque	470 lb-ft @ 2800 rpm
Carburetion	1 Carter 4-bbl
Transmission	3-speed automatic

Acceleration:
- 0–30 mph ... 4.0 sec.
- 0–40 mph ... 6.1 sec.
- 0–50 mph ... 9.0 sec.
- 0–60 mph ... 12.0 sec.
- 0–70 mph ... 16.3 sec.
- 0–80 mph ... 22.0 sec.

Mileage ... 15.10 mpg
80 mph to rest: panic stop ... 7.2 sec.

CADILLAC FLEETWOOD BROUGHAM

Price as tested:	$8,359.55
Length	227.5 in.
Height	56 in.
Width	80 in.
Curb weight	4600 lbs.
Wheelbase	133 in.
Engine type	OHV V-8
Displacement	429 cu. in.
Horsepower	340 bhp @ 4600 rpm
Torque	480 lb-ft @ 3000 rpm
Carburetion	1 Rochester 4-bbl
Transmission	3-speed automatic

Acceleration:
- 0–30 mph ... 3.4 sec.
- 0–40 mph ... 5.2 sec.
- 0–50 mph ... 6.9 sec.
- 0–60 mph ... 9.2 sec.
- 0–70 mph ... 11.8 sec.
- 0–80 mph ... 15.5 sec.

Mileage ... 10.53 mpg
80 mph to rest: panic stop ... 6.9 sec.

ROLLS-ROYCE SILVER CLOUD III

Price as tested:	$17,321
Length	212 in.
Height	64 in.
Width	75 in.
Curb weight	4500 lbs.
Wheelbase	123 in.
Engine type	OHV V-8
Displacement	380 cu. in.
Horsepower	n/a
Torque	n/a
Carburetion	2 SU
Transmission	4-speed automatic

Acceleration:
- 0–30 mph ... 4.3 sec.
- 0–40 mph ... 6.1 sec.
- 0–50 mph ... 8.9 sec.
- 0–60 mph ... 12.4 sec.
- 0–70 mph ... 15.5 sec.
- 0–80 mph ... 21.4 sec.

Mileage ... 14.54 mpg
80 mph to rest: panic stop ... 5.0 sec.

JAGUAR MARK X

Price as tested:	$6,990
Length	202 in.
Height	54.5 in.
Width	76 in.
Curb weight	4000 lbs.
Wheelbase	120 in.
Engine type	DOHC in-line 6
Displacement	255 cu. in.
Horsepower	265 bhp @ 5400 rpm
Torque	283 lb-ft @ 4500 rpm
Carburetion	3 SU
Transmission	3-speed automatic

Acceleration:
- 0–30 mph ... 4.1 sec.
- 0–40 mph ... 5.9 sec.
- 0–50 mph ... 7.9 sec.
- 0–60 mph ... 10.3 sec.
- 0–70 mph ... 14.0 sec.
- 0–80 mph ... 18.0 sec.

Mileage ... 15.28 mpg
80 mph to rest: panic stop ... 5.6 sec.

SIX LUXURY CARS CONTINUED

CONTINUED FROM PAGE 63

is the best of its kind, the wheel looks like something from a bus.

Another important feature is Cadillac's Comfort Control system—a combined heater/air conditioner that can be pre-set to the temperature of your taste and left there forever, keeping the interior at a uniform temperature day-in, day-out, winter and summer. Our only complaint was that it couldn't produce the same instant blast of frigid air that one gets from a typical, separate air conditioner (but it could bring the temperature down to a very pleasant minimum of 65° after a few minutes' running).

The Cadillac, contrary to enthusiast mythology, handles very well. It is agile, effortless, and predictable—always going where it's pointed without any fuss or surprises. Its ultimate handling potential falls short of the Mercedes 600 or the Jaguar 4.2 Sedan, but is noticeably better than the Rolls, the Imperial, or the Lincoln. We'd like to try a Cadillac with Koni shock absorbers and larger-section tires—these two very simple changes could elevate its already-acceptable road behavior to the first rank.

Cadillac's ride was the best of all six cars tested, as long as the roads were smooth, or uniformly rough—like well-maintained dirt or gravel. On potholes, and broken or undulating surfaces, the Cadillac shock absorbers were simply too soft, causing some uncomfortable pitching and wallowing. The only noise that found its way into the passenger compartment was some thumping from the rear wheels, and that wasn't too objectionable.

The Cadillac had the best power-to-weight ratio of the six cars tested, and its acceleration and throttle response were of the highest order. Much of this is due to the car's fine automatic transmission—a three-speed with torque converter—which is the best in the field. However, the brakes, like the standard shock absorbers, are not up to the high standard set by the rest of the package. While they were smooth and relatively fade-free in our test, they just didn't stop the car as fast as those on the Mercedes, the Rolls, the Jag, or the Lincoln—which is to say, not fast enough. We'd like to see Cadillac go to discs, or to a drum/disc combination as on the Lincoln. Their use of a dual master cylinder system is laudable, and it's a step in the right direction, but as presently sold the car doesn't have enough maximum-effort stopping power.

The Cadillac carried a greater variety of useful luxury equipment than any of the rest. Like the 600, it has a system that hydraulically locks or unlocks all four doors when either front door-lock is activated, and this is a great feature. It also has a cruise control-type throttle setting for turnpike driving—the best and easiest-to-use in our experience. Like every car in the group, except Rolls and Jaguar, Cadillac has an inside adjustment for the outside mirror. All knobs and switches are in easy reach, and there's no confusion about what they do or how they work.

The Cadillac is a fine automobile. Its fit and finish, silence and comfort, are equal to anybody's. Like all American cars of its ilk, it needs more brakes and better shock absorbers, but everything else is beyond criticism. In our estimation, Cadillac's great sales success is all that hurts its "image" as a prestige luxury car. If it was built in England just as it is, and they only built a thousand a year, the Cadillac Fleetwood would be an automotive legend selling very nicely, thank you, for about 15,000 dollars a copy. Barring that, they'll just have to settle for selling more cars than the other five put together.

The Lincoln Continental The Continental is the luxury car that almost made it. When the car was first introduced, it had a fresh look and a new concept that seemed tailor-made for the burgeoning luxury car market. It was a lovely thing to look at, and it was a nice size—smaller than either the Cadillac or the Imperial.

Our Lincoln test car still has some of that original flavor, but it's become longer, wider, heavier, less distinctive, more ponderous, less responsive, and it seems to be trying to look like last year's Cadillac. (All this must be very confusing for Chrysler styling chief Elwood Engel, who has succeeded by making Imperials and other Chrysler products look like Lincolns and other Ford products—so if next year's Lincoln looks like last year's Cadillac, then next year's Imperial will already be two years out-of-date).

All that notwithstanding, the Lincoln has managed to remain a very "nice" car. It has no glaring faults, but it has no undeniable charms, either. It finished third in our evaluation—beating the Rolls-Royce, the Imperial, and the Jaguar—largely because it is a much more effective statement of what a contemporary luxury car is supposed to be than they are. It was roomy and quiet, reasonably well-appointed, and it carried the full complement of luxury extras that we regard as mandatory in this class.

Entry and exit are excellent, and the ride is well up to modern standards. Passengers are quite comfortable, but the driver suffers a bit. The seats don't offer the same wide range of adjustment relative to the controls as on the Cadillac, for example, and none of the driving controls are quite up to the Cadillac's standard. Switches and small controls, as well as the instruments and instrument panel design, have a kind of low-priced-three look that seems somewhat out of place. There are more luxurious trim packages available, but this one wasn't too great.

In performance, the Lincoln is the opposite of the Cadillac. Where the Cadillac goes fast, with some reluctance to stop, the Lincoln doesn't go very fast at all, but stops like crazy. Ford is to be sincerely congratulated for their decision to lead the industry in accepting the absolute necessity of better brakes. Kelsey-Hayes ventilated discs are standard on the Lincoln and the Thunderbird, and optional on the Mustang—a fact that we heartily applaud.

By itself, the Lincoln is a good example of an expensive, contemporary American car. Only in a direct comparison does its acceleration seem a bit sluggish, its handling vague. Only when you've just jumped out of a really good driver's seat do you find yourself fidgeting and wiggling around in the Lincoln. Like some table wines, the Lincoln is a good car: not a great car, but a good car.

The Rolls-Royce Silver Cloud The keener American enthusiast, with his particularly virulent Anglophilia, will never swallow this, but the Rolls-Royce Silver Cloud is exactly what the same enthusiast has always called the Cadillac—an automotive status symbol with relatively few *genuine* product-benefits to justify its cost. The craftsmanship is worth quite a lot, as is the high quality of the materials used. The Rolls will undoubtedly survive after most of its upstart competitors have been consigned to the scrap heap, but what the Rolls buyer is really paying for is the instant respectability of the radiator shell, and the social ac-

SIX LUXURY CARS CONTINUED

ceptance it bestows upon its owner.

The Rolls-Royce is probably the most overrated car in the world. It *is* silent. It *is* smooth. And it *is* beautifully put together. But it is also—at best—only a superb example of what modern manufacturing technology and a spare-no-expense philosophy can do for a 1939 Packard. Driving the Rolls was exactly like driving a beautifully restored classic—one applauds the craftsmanship and the fine materials used, while sadly acknowledging the functional limitations of obsolescence.

Entry and exit are difficult because it's a bit of a climb to the door sill, and because the doors are narrow and the seats high. There is no power seat adjustment, no steering wheel adjustment, no inside adjustment for the outside mirror, very little room inside (which is strange, in view of the car's great exterior dimensions), minimum luggage space, suspension that betrays every secret of the road surface, and an air-conditioning installation that is too obviously an afterthought.

The instrument panel is covered with little switches that cannot be identified without reference to the manual, and although the instruments are the black dials with white markings that we all love so well, they are cluttered and confusing. The transmission is very harsh in shifting, and its quadrant (N432R) is nonstandard and features no PARK position.

Two components impressed us—the engine and the brakes. The engine is described by Eric Nielssen on page 67. Though not a stormer, by any means, it delivers its thrust with the silence and smoothness of a steam turbine. It is wonderfully smooth and silent, and performs its function in exactly the way that Rolls-Royce folklore promises.

The brakes are absolutely amazing. Again, they have been described in detail elsewhere, but their performance is truly fantastic. Only the Mercedes 600, with four-wheel discs, was able to stop faster from eighty mph, and it slewed a mite in doing so. The Rolls was almost as fast in deceleration, and it was dead smooth and straight as an arrow. It felt like the car had run into a giant feather mattress and was simply being forced to a stop from the outside. Great brakes!

The handling, unfortunately, evokes no such praise. The steering was dead and unresponsive, and there was a rather unusual tendency toward roll-steer (a change in turning radius caused by the turning vehicle's shifting weight), which made it virtually impossible to hurry the car on a winding road, or to negotiate a simple slalom maneuver that the other five cars managed with relative ease. Similarly, the Rolls did not seem very pleasant to any of us at sustained high cruising speeds.

We will obviously incur the wrath of the purist horde with these sentiments, but our staff is unanimous in its disappointment with the Rolls-Royce. It is *not* a modern car, and though it has smoothness, silence, good brakes, beautiful workmanship, and reasonable comfort for no more than four, the car is distinguished only by its traditional appearance—its good qualities have been available in automobiles since World War I. The Rolls will provide its owner with all these benefits and probably outlive him in the bargain, but it won't do what the Mercedes or the Cadillac or the Lincoln will, no matter how much wood it has inside.

The Imperial LeBaron The Imperial—much like the Rolls—feels like a classic car. It seems huge. Its styling accentuates this vastness and tends to intimidate the driver when he's forced to drive it in constricted places that could mar its flanks. On the turnpike, the Imperial rolls along effortlessly and is quite pleasant, but it needs those wide open spaces.

Getting into the front seat is easy enough, but the rear is tough—not at all like the Lincoln with its wide-swinging, backward-opening rear doors that make it so easy. Once in, the interior is quite comfortable, though the range of seat and steering wheel adjustments (except on bucket seat models) is well below that of the Cadillac. Instrumentation is very complete, and the controls are easily used and well-marked. The air conditioning installation was poor though, consisting of unattractive, adjustable plastic vents in the cowl. There was general agreement among the staff members that the Imperial's appointments gave the least feeling of genuine elegance of the six, being more tinsel and flash than real quality. Finish and quality of workmanship were also below standard for the group, though probably acceptable in more typical, bread-and-butter sedans. Again, the reader is reminded that this car was not the top of the Imperial line.

The other area that scored against our Imperial was its general performance—both braking and acceleration put the car right at the bottom of the class. The brakes were not only limited in stopping power, they were grabby and directionally unstable.

All this is especially unfortunate, in view of the really fine job Chrysler Corporation has done with its other car lines. The Chryslers, particularly, are very handsome, and have a lithe feeling and a responsiveness that makes them very desirable indeed. Somehow, the Imperial seems to lag about five years behind other Chrysler cars.

The Jaguar 4.2 (formerly Mark X) Sedan The Jaguar was operating under a distinct handicap in this league. It is far more sports car than luxury car, and although this is a combination to warm the heart of every red-blooded enthusiast, it will not find favor with the well-heeled burgher who leans toward the Mercedes or the Cadillac. Fortunately Jaguar's U.S. sales projections for this model are extremely modest, so that they can afford to wait for that "Mr. Right" to come along.

The Jag was the only one of our six test cars to share the distinction of four-wheel disc brakes and four-wheel independent suspension with the Mercedes. These make it a very sporty machine; so much so, that the driver is really hard-pressed to find any significant benefits in the 4.2 Sedan over its more-compact brother, the Jaguar 3.8-S.

It has no provision for factory-installed air-conditioning, so that one must either do without, or learn to live with a cobbled-up dealer installation. The heater controls are very confusing, and the heater is not very effective—especially when compared to the other five cars tested. The Borg-Warner automatic transmission seems to suffer considerable power-loss, and the shifting action is as rough as on the Rolls or the Mercedes, except at full throttle, when it becomes very smooth. It starts in second gear for normal use and, like the Rolls-Royce, its selector lever must be moved to low range before first can be engaged (the Mercedes can be started in first by simply depressing the accelerator all the way). It also shares a very noisy electric window system with the Rolls, and has no power seats.

On the subject of seats, the Jag's are basically similar to those used in every big Jaguar since the early Mark VII. The front seat-backs are infinitely adjustable, but the seat cushions are thin, a bit slippery, and seem to slope downward toward the front—resulting in an uneasy feeling that one is gradually slipping down and forward as the trip progresses, possibly to disappear completely beneath the steering wheel.

Although the Jaguar feels heavy and a little ponderous, its handling is really very good—probably the best in this class—when measured in terms of maximum cornering power and evasive capability. Jaguar's power-steering is definitely superior to the others. Much smaller than the others, with generally stiffer suspension, the Jag can be twisted around obstacles and through slalom-like maneuvers very briskly —although it required slightly more effort than the others.

The instrumentation is excellent and the small controls—mostly crisp, on-off toggle switches, are terrific.

There is no inside adjustment for the outside mirror, but the steering wheel can be adjusted for reach by turning a collar on the underside of the wheel-hub. The quality and type of materials used in the interior are —for all practical purposes—just like the Rolls-Royce (like all English sedans, for that matter). The *only* serious complaint we have with the interior are the seats and the spartan lack of luxury accessory equipment. The ride is harsh, with some pitching, but the man who buys the 4.2 Sedan is probably going to enjoy the handling more than he'll miss a boulevard ride.

Given a full selection of comfort and convenience accessories, better seats, and the Cadillac's three-speed automatic transmission, the Jaguar 4.2 could be a uniquely desirable combination of sports car and luxury sedan. As it is, it occupies a sort of middle ground, its appeal limited more to the man-who-wants-a-more-expensive-Jaguar, than to the typical luxury car prospect.

Conclusion There they are—the Mercedes-Benz 600, the Cadillac Fleetwood, the Lincoln Continental, the Rolls-Royce Silver Cloud, the Imperial LeBaron, and the Jaguar 4.2 Sedan—in order of our preference and their performance.

Usually, the never-ending triumph of progress over tradition leaves one feeling a little sad and empty. This time, though, we admit to a curiously pleasant feeling of elation. Maybe we've made a little progress of our own.... **C/D**

TECH SIX *(Cont. from p. 69)*

The only other unusual hydraulic application on these cars is found on the Lincoln which fits a Trico system to operate the windshield wipers.

Today, with assembly plants all across the country, it's worth noting that each of the three American luxury models is made exclusively in one single plant. Cadillac, for example, is the only GM car which can make that claim. This means that production quality can be held at a consistent level (hopefully high) for all cars of a given make. It's also pertinent to note that Cadillac is the only one of the six that's available in a comprehensive range of body types and price ranges which accounts in part for its overwhelming sales position in the class.

Lincoln was the first American car to make the offer of a two-year, 24,000-mile warranty, and each vehicle is given a 15-mile test run before leaving the factory. Rolls-Royce has the longest pre-delivery testing program, with each automobile logging 50 miles on chassis rollers and 150 miles on the open road. These examples are typical of the pains most of the luxury car manufacturers take to insure proper assembly in their products.

The three American cars are among an exclusive group of domestic automobiles built in a single factory. This means that tight control can be kept on quality and assembly procedures and is doubtless a factor in the general level of workmanship on the cars. Jaguar and Mercedes-Benz both utilize similar ultramodern industrial techniques in manufacturing the Mark X and the 600, and it is interesting to note that Mercedes is fully tooled to produce 5000 of the 600s per month, though demand is never expected to exceed 150 per month. A very modern concept, indeed.

Conversely, the Rolls-Royce is one of the few cars in the world that truly deserves its reputation for "old-world craftsmanship." The automobile is assembled with the kind of loving care that the owner of every fine automobile likes to think he paid for. But alas, this is the work of devoted, if fusty, old craftsmen, and only the production techniques used in the Rolls-Royce automobile plant permit this splendid consumption of time. You can be sure, however, that considerably more contemporary processes are utilized by Rolls in its aircraft jet engine plant, and some of them will doubtless be drawn upon when Crewe's anticipated new model makes its bow. **C/D**

CADILLAC

(Continued from page 25)

The press-button, instant-action screenwasher and three-speed wipers (overlapping, mark you) should keep the huge tinted screen clear as crystal in anything but a deluge.

Two separate air-conditioning systems — heating/demisting and refrigeration—work perfectly, and adjustable angled slats allow you to direct the warming or cooling airflow to almost any position inside the car.

Driver's Angle

The range of seating adjustments is so varied that anyone—long or short, fat or thin—can select the ideal driving position for his frame.

And it's done with incredible ease, by operating electric controls which raise or lower the front seat, move it to and fro, tilt it up or down, until you are satisfied.

I found several comfortable positions, depending on my driving mood. But I also found my rear vision somewhat limited by the smallish internal mirror and was glad of the external mirrors—the left-hand one being adjustable from inside without lowering the window!

One other complaint on the score of visibility: the sloping windscreen pillars are on the thick side by modern standards. But this was probably deemed necessary to ensure that the roof is adequately supported in the absence of central pillars.

The selector panel for the four-speed Hydra-Matic transmission lists two "drive" positions; the left-hand one gives the full four speeds, while the right-hand position cuts out high gear and is recommended for use in hilly country (for the sporting owner?).

The Caddy, of course, is normally a left-hand drive vehicle. The conversion to right-hand drive has been done very neatly, except for one thing: The foot-operated parking brake is set too close to the throttle and tends to crowd the driver's all-important right foot, which does all the work in "automatics."

It's a pity that such an obvious point should have been overlooked, especially when the designers have taken such pains to make the driver comfortable. They've even provided him with remote controls to lock or unlock all doors and raise or lower all windows without ungainly reaching.

Along with all these gimmicks, which fascinated both me and my three-year-old daughter (she was a sucker for the disappearing aerial), there's a magic-eye headlight dipper, which automatically puts your headlights on low beam when you meet other traffic at night.

This control is so sensitive that once it politely dipped our headlights to a reflective road sign!

On the Road

Being conscious of the car's value, I handled it somewhat sedately during the four-day test period. Even when going over my regular mountain course, I tried to forget my sporting instincts, pretending I was a tycoon in a hurry—well, a moderate hurry—and kept to the four-speed side of the transmission quadrant.

John McKittrick, who logged the run for me, was amazed at the big car's agility—but had he been driving he'd have realised just how simple it was to hurl 45cwt. of Caddy through the bends.

The 3½ turns lock-to-lock, plus power steering, plus a gross 345 b.h.p., plus a commendably flat and stable ride, made my job easy.

A limited-slip diff—offered as optional equipment, according to the factory's surprisingly scanty instruction book—would have helped greatly up the hill; but even so, the heavy car shot up the climb in 2min. 33sec. to the accompaniment of appropriate jet noises.

Despite my restrained driving, it recorded 50 m.p.h for the circuit—an average many saloons would envy. Had I used the three-speed drive position and given the car its head, I am sure it could have averaged between 52 and 53 m.p.h.

On a long-distance run, say Sydney to Adelaide, I would imagine the Caddy would really shine, and any sort of car would have to motor really hard to keep up with it.

I used the normal 24lb. pressure in the big 8.00 by 15in. tyres—but for sustained speeds in excess of 75 m.p.h a pressure of 28lb. is suggested. Obviously, G.M. had turnpike derbies in mind when giving this advice.

With the windows shut, 80 m.p.h was quite silent, and even the maximum of 110 gave little indication of our velocity.

It was only when braking from speeds "over the ton" that the brakes seemed a trifle worried. Over the mountain circuit, where high speeds aren't possible, the brakes coped with the great weight uncomplainingly.

Perhaps G.M., who can obviously make a car that's equal to any in the world, will follow the proud Daimler-Benz factory's example and fit the unbeatable British disc brakes to make this fine chariot even better than it is.

And it IS a fine chariot — make no mistake about that. The ride, the handling, the overall performance and comfort — plus such minor detail touches as a warning light that goes on when you open the boot, and red reflectors inside the doors, to warn other traffic when these are opened — show what Detroit can achieve when it wants to, and when cost is no object.

To all this you can add a surprisingly moderate thirst for petrol. I thought we'd be lucky to get 10 m.p.g. from such a heavy car with massive 6½-litre engine, but consumption worked out at 12.2 m.p.g., despite the arduous test course.

No wonder the Cadillac is the world's top-selling "car of distinction."

FOOTNOTE: This particular car had previously been running on premium-grade pump petrol until recently — and disliking it. It now normally uses a mixture of methyl-benzine and super (1 to 3), but for this test we fed it 100 octane fuel.

The chauffeurs report the Caddy to be a different car on either MB or 100-octane — not surprising, considering the engine's 10.5 to 1 compression ratio! ● ● ●

GM's crown jewel

Cadillac's casual car, the De Ville convertible, provides the last word in carefree driving

by John Ethridge
Technical Editor

CADILLAC OCCUPIES an enviable position in its field. Not only does it outsell all domestic cars in its class combined, but it's often considered in the same league with foreign luxury cars costing over three times as much.

When you look into the underlying reasons, you find it isn't quality alone that accounts for Cadillac's enormous prestige. The car's quality is undeniably good — it compares favorably with that of any automobile at any price. But the makers realize that, by itself, quality won't guarantee continued leadership in the luxury field. They've long known that things bordering on the abstract, such as association (fine jewelry) and distinctiveness (even with all insignia removed, it's instantly recognizable as a Cadillac), help assure concrete benefits like high resale value and owner loyalty. These two things are mutually regenerating and are what really account for the unassailable position Cadillac has enjoyed for quite some time. The Cadillac people have carefully nurtured these things in their advertising and by such devices as affixing the original purchaser's signature to the car.

For the sake of identification, the current model has to look like those of past years. In fact, if you go back a decade, you'll find today's car bears a marked resemblance to the 1955 model. Yet there's nothing antiquated about it. From both styling and engineering standpoints, it's as contemporary as anything on the road. The most significant styling change for 1965 is that the famous fins, which have adorned Cadillacs for 17 years, have receded into the rear fender line.

A new frame, the first in nine years, heads the list of engineering changes. Like those of other GM cars, the frame is a perimeter type, and it gives a weight saving of about 300 pounds over the old one. For the past several years, most Cadillacs have been sold with several hundred pounds of accessories. Weight was getting out of hand. The tires, brakes, and suspension will welcome the relief. Those of you who feel a Cadillac *should* be heavy shouldn't worry. It still weighs plenty and has one of the most favorable sprung/unsprung weight ratios (for good ride) of any car.

The engine's been moved farther forward in the new frame, reducing the size of the transmission hump. The bulk of the Comfort Control heating/air-conditioning unit now occupies underhood space instead of being in the passenger compartment. This results in far more knee room for the front-seat passengers and simplifies servicing the unit.

The history of Cadillac is to a large extent the story of a list of well engineered accessories available as extras on the car. Foremost is the Comfort Control unit. The heating and air-conditioning systems are combined and are controlled by a "brain" on the instrument panel. In engineering language, it's a *servo-mechanism*. It senses the difference between the temperature you've dialed and that of the passenger compartment, then gives the necessary commands to appropriate parts of the system to adjust the temperature. In addition to turning the compressor and hot water on and off, the system also opens and closes various ducts. At one phase, both the heater and air conditioner go on simultaneously to de-humidify the air.

We approached the Comfort Control with a certain amount of skepticism at first, because we appreciate the problems involved in making a system like this — that sells for less than $500 and still does all the things it's supposed to do. We were pleasantly surprised to find it worked perfectly under all tests we devised. It did tend to hunt (alternately blew hot and cold) when ambient temperature reached that set on the dial. This, though, isn't a real complaint. Changing the set temperature slightly cured it if we didn't want to shut it off and open the windows.

Besides the automatic headlight-

Numerous power-consuming accessories call for very busy engine compartment. Extra capacity of cross-flow radiator and condenser stops overheating.

Smooth, powerful "429" V-8 comes already broken in, uses Carter AFB or Rochester four-barrel carb.

GLASS REAR WINDOW CURES MAJOR CONVERTIBLE BUGABOO. TOP'S TAUTLY ATTACHED TO EACH BOW TO PREVENT BALLOONING AT HIGH SPEEDS.

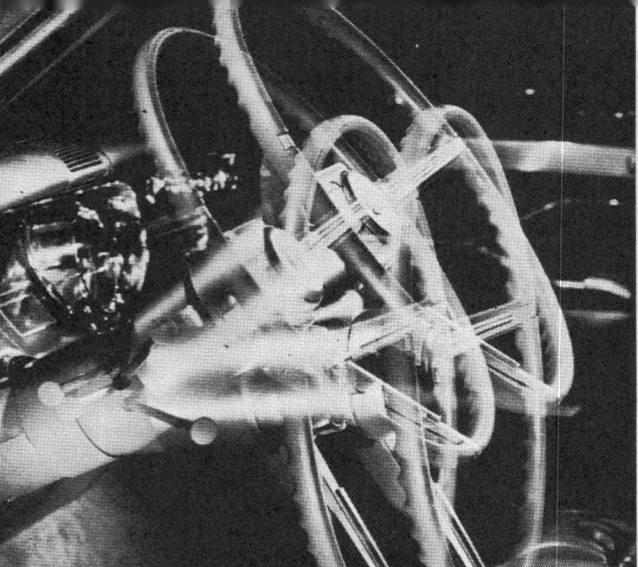

Just a few positions possible with the Saginaw swiveler. There ought to be at least one to suit every driver.

New layout of engine and accessories adds to roominess and comfort inside. All manually operated controls can be reached with seat belt fastened.

dimmer control, our test car had the Twilight Sentinel. This automatically turns on the headlights when sunlight falls below a certain level. It incorporates a variable delay so you can park the car, turn off the ignition, and the lights will stay on until you, say, find the keyhole and are safely inside your house.

Between the four-way bucket seat in our test car and the tilting and telescoping steering wheel, most everyone can find a comfortable driving position. The bucket seats are perforated for ventilation and are among the most comfortable we've sat on. They cost $187.85, including a console with locking compartment.

We almost forgot to mention one optional extra ($80.65) our test car had, so unobtrusively did it do its job. The Automatic Level Control, which works with gas pressure on the rear shocks, quickly restores the status quo when a change in loading causes the rear end to sag.

Cadillac continues with its powerful and — for its size — economical 429-cubic-inch V-8. Overall average for our 888-mile test was 12.1 mpg, which covered mostly city driving. A freeway trip at steady legal speed gave 14.2 mpg. This was, of course, with the air conditioning and 3.21 axle. The standard 2.94 axle should yield phenomenal fuel economy. Performance runs dropped mileage to 10.5 — our low for the test.

Although stopping distances weren't unusually short, the big 12-inch brakes showed no signs of fade during turn-arounds after our acceleration runs. About seven out of 10 cars we test won't get through these turn-arounds without some degree of fade.

As for the rest of the Cadillac line, all models except the Series 75 are pretty much as we've described the De Ville. The nine-passenger 75s continue with last year's X-braced tubular frame and horizontal headlamps. Also, the 75s retain the two-piece driveshaft, while other models have gone to a single shaft. What was formerly called the Series 62 is now more euphoniously referred to as the Calais.

You always get that extra that comes with every Cadillac at no extra cost: It's an unmistakable status symbol in the eyes of the well-to-do as well as the man in the street. With this on top of good engineering and distinctive styling, what more could you ask for in a luxury car? /MT

CADILLAC DE VILLE
2-door, 5-passenger convertible

OPTIONS ON TEST CAR: Comfort Control, bucket seats, AM-FM radio, automatic level control, electric seats, electric windows, power door locks, adjustable steering wheel, controlled differential.
BASE PRICE: $5639
PRICE AS TESTED: $7494.60 (plus tax and license)
ODOMETER READING AT START OF TEST: 4785 miles
RECOMMENDED ENGINE RED LINE: 5200 rpm

PERFORMANCE
ACCELERATION (2 aboard)
- 0-30 mph .... 3.3 secs
- 0-45 mph 6.0
- 0-60 mph 9.5

PASSING TIMES AND DISTANCES
- 40-60 mph .... 5.2 secs., 382 ft.
- 50-70 mph .... 6.0 secs., 528 ft.

Standing start ¼-mile 17.2 secs. and 82 mph
Speeds in gears @ 4400 rpm (shift point)
- 1st .... 45 mph   3rd .... 113 mph
- 2nd .... 76 mph   (observed)

Speedometer Error on Test Car
- Car's speedometer reading 32 48 54 64 74 85
- Weston electric speedometer 30 45 50 60 70 80

Observed mph per 1000 rpm in top gear .... 25.2 mph
Stopping Distances — from 30 mph, 37 ft.; from 60 mph, 184 ft.

SPECIFICATIONS FROM MANUFACTURER

Engine
Ohv V-8
Bore: 4.13 ins.
Stroke: 4.0 ins.
Displacement: 429 cu. ins.
Compression ratio: 10.5:1
Horsepower: 340 @ 4600 rpm
Horsepower per cubic inch: 0.79
Torque: 480 lbs.-ft. @ 3000 rpm
Carburetion: 1 4-bbl.
Ignition: 12-volt coil

Gearbox
Turbo Hydra-Matic 3-speed automatic with variable-vane torque converter; column-mounted lever

Driveshaft
1-piece, open tube

Differential
Hypoid, limited slip
Standard ratio: 3.21:1

Suspension
Front: Independent, with coil springs, upper A-arm, SLA with strut, tubular shocks, anti-roll bar
Rear: Rigid axle, coil springs, 4-link arms, tubular shocks

Steering
Ball nut sector with coaxial power assist
Turning diameter: 44.7 ft.
Turns lock to lock: 3.7

Wheels and Tires
15 x 6JK 5-lug, slotted steel disc wheels
9.00 x 15 4-ply tubeless whitewall tires

Brakes
Hydraulic, duo-servo, self-adjusting, dual master cylinder
Front: 12-in. dia. x 2.5 ins. wide
Rear: 12-in. dia. x 2.5 ins. wide
Effective lining area: 203.6 sq. ins.
Swept drum area: 377.0 sq. ins.

Body and Frame
Separate steel body on perimeter frame
Wheelbase: 129.5 ins.
Track: front, 62.5 ins.; rear, 62.5 ins.
Overall length: 224.0 ins.
Overall width: 79.9 ins.
Overall height: 54.6 ins.
Curb weight: 4820 lbs.

WIDENED TREAD AND LOW-PROFILE 9.00 X 15 TIRES IMPROVE CORNERING STABILITY, ALREADY RELATIVELY GOOD FOR A 4800-POUND CAR.

De Ville convertible stows top within body outline, without sacrificing any trunk room.

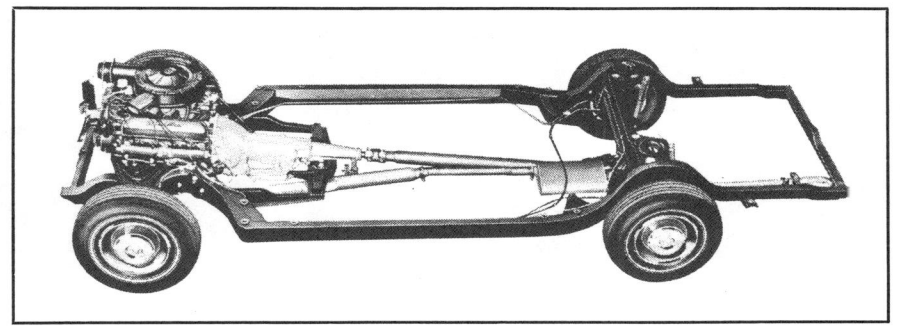

New weight-saving perimeter frame mounts engine farther forward. Four-link rear suspension's been redesigned. Two-piece driveshaft's been abandoned for one-piece unit.

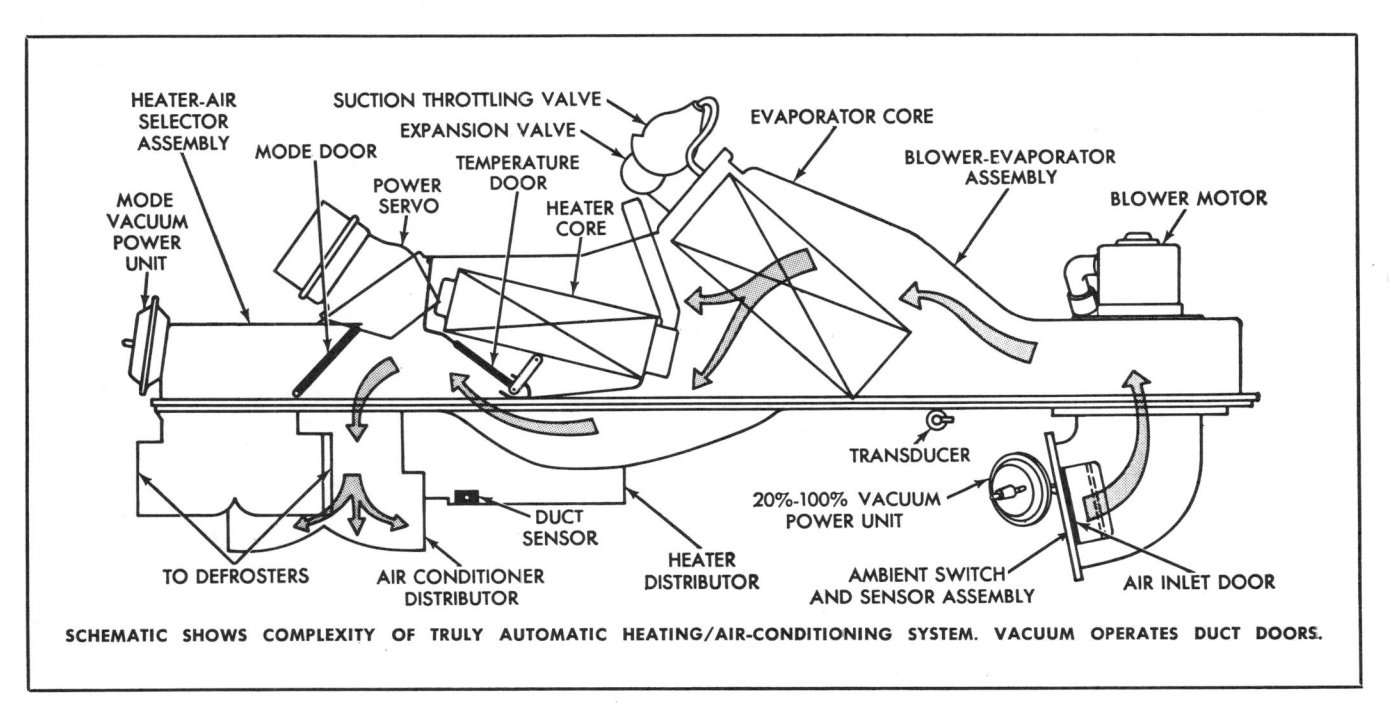

SCHEMATIC SHOWS COMPLEXITY OF TRULY AUTOMATIC HEATING/AIR-CONDITIONING SYSTEM. VACUUM OPERATES DUCT DOORS.

CADILLAC

Cadillac presents for 1966 12 body models to meet the individual preferences of every fine car owner: the Calais coupe, sedan, and hardtop sedan; the DeVille convertible, coupe, sedan, and hardtop sedan; the Fleetwood, Eldorado convertible, Sixty Special sedan, Brougham, nine-passenger sedan and limousine.

Cadillac styling for 1966 is in the nature of refinements on the theme introduced last year. A new grille with a horizontal bar in the center wraps around the inside of the front fenders.

Fleetwood 75 sedan and limousine the wheelbase is 149.8 inches.

The powerplant for Cadillac cars includes a 340-horsepower engine, providing higher horsepower per pound of engine weight than any other competitive motor car. Displacement is 429 cubic inches. The Cadillac transmission is the Turbo Hydra-Matic box which consists of a fully automatic torque converter with variable stator.

As expected, Cadillac offers many power accessories: Optional at extra cost, the Cadillac tilt and telescope

Cadillac Calais hardtop sedan.

Cadillac Fleetwood Brougham sedan.

New taillights and bumpers that house the license plate are the major changes to the car. The driver's turn signal indicators are now integrated with the front fenders instead of being an applied chrome piece.

Biggest change is that the 75 sedan and limousine have been restyled and redesigned, including the change to a perimeter frame to match the rest of the line. However, a two-piece driveshaft is retained in these models. The automatic level control, formerly optional on all models, is now standard on all 75's.

A new variable ratio steering heads the list of engineering changes. The steering ratio gets faster with increasing lock. A new option for 1966 is the electrically heated front seats. Turned on manually, four carbon cloth pads warm up to 85-105°F to take the chill off. The unit goes off automatically as soon as the heater fan comes on, or you can turn it off using the control. The wheelbase on all models is 129.5 inches except on the Fleetwood 60 Special sedan and Brougham which carries a 133-inch wheelbase. On the

Cadillac DeVille convertible.

steering wheel, Cadillac cruise control, Cadillac power door locks, Cadillac remote-control trunk lock, Cadillac Guidematic (power headlamp control), Cadillac Twilight Sentinel (automatic headlamp timer), and Cadillac automatic level control. In addition, Cadillac offers the automatic climate control air conditioner heater system which is available at extra cost, standard on 75 models. Also offered as extras, the Cadillac rear-window de-fogger, glare-free glass, controlled differential.

1966 CADILLAC SPECIFICATIONS

CADILLAC CAR MODELS: Cadillac presents for 1966 twelve body models to meet the individual preferences of every fine car owner: the Calais Coupe, Sedan and Hardtop Sedan; the De Ville Convertible, Coupe, Sedan and Hardtop Sedan; the Fleetwood Eldorado Convertible, Coupe and Hardtop Sedan de Ville; the Fleetwood Eldorado Convertible, Sixty Special Sedan, Brougham, Nine-Passenger Sedan and Limousine.

BUCKET FRONT SEATS: (Includes locking padded console compartment between seats.) Available at extra cost on the De Ville Convertible, Coupe and Hardtop Sedan de Ville and at no extra cost on the Fleetwood Eldorado Convertible. New Recliner feature available for passenger side, includes new headrest. Driver's seat also has headrest.

WHEELBASE: 129.5" except 133.0" on Fleetwood Sixty Special Sedan and Brougham and 149.8" on Fleetwood Seventy-Five Sedan and Limousine.

OVER-ALL LENGTH: 224.0" except 227.5" for Fleetwood Sixty Special Sedan and Brougham and 244.5" for Fleetwood Seventy-Five Sedan and Limousine.

ENGINE: The 340-horsepower Cadillac engine provides higher horsepower per pound of engine weight than any competitive motor car. Displacement, 429 cubic inches; compression ratio, 10.5 to 1; bore and stroke, 4.13" x 4.0". Features include an automatic idle control valve to assure smooth engine idling even under sustained idling conditions; highly sensitive automatic choke control for maximum performance and economy; dual fuel filters, one in fuel tank, one in engine compartment for maximum protection against dirt particles or water; full-flow oil filter, single coaxial resonator exhaust system. Pistons, connecting rods and crankshaft design contribute to fast starting and improved acceleration. Maximum torque, 480 foot-pounds.

ELECTRICAL SYSTEM: 12-volt including a new 13-plate battery with rubber separators for long battery life; high-torque starting motor; high-capacity 42-amp. generator (55-amp. on Air Conditioner-equipped cars and Fleetwood Seventy-Five models) and precise, high-voltage, lifetime-lubricated distributor. Waterproofed ignition system.

CADILLAC TURBO HYDRA-MATIC TRANSMISSION: Fully automatic torque converter (with variable stator except on Fleetwood 75 models) combined with step-gear shifts, Low, Intermediate and High. In any forward gear or reverse, engine torque is multiplied up to two times by torque converter.

PROPELLER SHAFT: One-piece with CV (constant velocity) joints. Two-piece with CV-joints on Fleetwood 75.

REAR AXLE: Hypoid; differential housing offset to provide straight-line drive. Numerically low rear axle ratio of 2.94 to 1 (3.21 to 1 with Air Conditioner-equipped and 75 models and optional on other models) means quiet and economical engine performance.

FRAME: Cadillac perimeter frame provides high torsional rigidity. It has also permitted moving the engine forward resulting in a smaller, lower floor tunnel and increased interior roominess.

FRONT SUSPENSION: Tension-strut design. Strut rods mounted to control arms and through heavy rubber bushings to front frame crossmember, control fore and aft movement of wheels while absorbing impacts and road noise. Spherical joints permit positioning control arms to keep car level and resist front-end dive during braking. Front springs are helical-coil type with shock absorber mounted within each coil spring.

REAR SUSPENSION: Cadillac four-link rear suspension utilizes two lower and two upper control arms. Splay mounting of upper arms resists sideways movement and minimizes outward lean on turns or curves. Rubber bushings for control arms assure a quiet ride and cushion impacts.

SHOCK ABSORBERS: Hydraulic, direct-acting shock absorbers with a Freon gas-filled nylon envelope replacing conventional air space in reservoir. Thus shock absorber efficiency cannot be lost through aeration of fluid. Fluid itself is high-viscosity, airplane-type impervious to temperature changes. Nylon ring around piston absorbs abrasive particles and prevents scoring of cylinder walls.

CADILLAC POWER STEERING: Standard on all models, Cadillac Power Steering has a flexible coupling in the steering shaft which prevents transmission of vibration, road shock and noise to the car interior. Rotary valve and large pump capacity provide minimum steering effort. Ball joints permanently sealed for lifetime lubrication. New variable steering ratio (fixed ratio on 75 models) and 38.5° turning angle contribute to fast response and small turning diameter. Variable ratio reduces steering effort as much as one-third for extreme cornering and parking.

CADILLAC POWER BRAKES: Standard equipment on all models, Cadillac Power Brakes have a split-hydraulic system. Separate piston and fluid reservoir for front and rear brakes permits one set working in the event either set fails. A direct, push-rod-activated, vacuum-power cylinder with self-contained vacuum reservoir provides instant response. Finned front and rear drums for maximum cooling. Sintered-iron, self-lubricating wheel brake cylinder pistons for increased life and corrosion resistance. Flange on front brake backing plates for increased protection against entry of water or dirt. Brakes adjust automatically to compensate for lining wear. Diaphragm seal on cover of master brake cylinder reservoirs prevents contamination of brake fluid.

CADILLAC PARKING BRAKE: Parking brake is automatically vacuum-released when engine is started and Turbo Hydra-Matic lever placed in any forward or reverse gear. It serves as a true auxiliary brake, since it can be applied without locking in position under above conditions.

DIRECTIONAL SIGNALS: Standard equipment. Front signal (and parking) lamps have white lens with yellow filter, thus showing amber only when illuminated.

CORNERING LIGHTS: Standard equipment. Located on side of front fenders behind headlamps, Cadillac Cornering Lights are activated by directional signal switch when headlamps are ON. They project a fan-shaped beam from the side of the car, thus illuminating roadside as an aid to nighttime driving when cornering.

BACKUP LIGHTS: Standard equipment.

OUTSIDE REAR VIEW MIRROR: Standard equipment. Remote-control adjustment located inside of car for maximum convenience.

POWER WINDOW REGULATORS AND SIX-WAY FRONT SEAT ADJUSTMENT: Cadillac power window regulators, featuring a 3-position master switch with emergency override, and power horizontal front seat adjustment are provided as standard equipment on the De Ville Convertible, Coupe de Ville and Sedans de Ville, Fleetwood 60 Special Sedan and Brougham and Fleetwood 75 models. A power-operated vertical and seat angle adjustment available at extra cost except on Fleetwood Limousine is standard for Fleetwood Eldorado (angle adjustment, driver's side only for bucket seats.)

The six-way front seat adjustment and power window regulators are optional at extra cost on Calais Sedans and Coupe.

Power-operated vent window regulators are standard on the Fleetwood Eldorado, 60 Special Sedan and Brougham and an extra-cost option on all other models equipped with power window regulators.

ADDITIONAL CADILLAC POWER ACCESSORIES: Optional at extra cost. Cadillac Tilt and Telescope Steering Wheel, Cadillac Cruise Control, Cadillac Power Door Locks, Cadillac Remote-control Trunk Lock, Cadillac Guide-Matic (power headlamp control), Cadillac Twilight Sentinel (automatic headlamp timer) and Cadillac Automatic Level Control.*

CADILLAC AIR CONDITIONER-HEATER: The Automatic Climate Control Air Conditioner Heater System available at extra cost (standard on 75 models)—automatically maintains temperature selected and adjusts for humidity, year 'round, without necessity of resetting. Fleetwood 75 models have separate systems for front and rear compartments including separate controls in rear compartment, and two adjustable cool air outlets located overhead at each side of the rear compartment.

CADILLAC REAR WINDOW DE-FOGGER: Optional at extra cost.

CADILLAC SOFT RAY GLASS: Optional at extra cost.

CADILLAC CONTROLLED DIFFERENTIAL: Optional at extra cost. Directs driving force to rear wheel with better traction for surer mobility in mud, sand, snow, gravel and on other slippery road surfaces.

TIRES: Low-pressure, tubeless tires of special compound and tread design. 2-ply; 4-ply rating (4-ply; 8-ply rating on Fleetwood 75). Size 8.20 x 15 on Fleetwood 75 cars and 9.00 x 15 on all other models.**

GASOLINE TANK: Approximately 26 gallons.

LUBRICATION: Pre-packed suspension and steering connections for minimum maintenance; engine crankcase capacity, 5 qts. including filter.

*Standard on all Fleetwood models.   **Whitewalls standard on Fleetwood Eldorado Convertible, extra cost on all other models.

GO WEST YOUNG MAN...
IN A 1966 CADILLAC!

CADILLAC BRAKES ARE BRAWNY STOPPERS, GOOD ENOUGH TO PRECLUDE A SWITCH TO DISCS IN FUTURE. DUAL MASTER CYLINDERS STANDARD.

3,000 MILES OF ELEGANCE, LUXURY, AND ADJUSTABILITY IS ENOUGH TO CONVERT ALMOST ANYBODY

by Robert E. McVay,
Associate Editor

"GO EAST, young man," our editor instructed, "and head back West with a 1966 Cadillac." That's how it all started. Some 3,000 miles later, we returned with this top luxury machine, very much impressed with the car and with the way it's put together.

Our personal tour of Cadillac's vastly expanded facilities (they've increased working space by 50% and have added tons of new testing equipment) impressed on us the fact that this is a thoroughly tested automobile, probably far more refined than certain other top luxury cars from across the pond whose makers couldn't begin to afford the facilities Cadillac has.

Take for instance their one-of-a-kind Road Simulator. It holds a car on four hydraulic pistons and can be programed to simulate any road surface, anywhere in the world. It finds out in 30 seconds what it took hours to find out on the old mechanical shakers. Cost of this device was $250,000. In addition, we saw a vast array of dynamometers, hot and cold rooms, wind tunnels, and component-testing setups.

Watching the assembly line was another surprise. At maximum pace, 50 cars a day is tops, with two shifts. Care is taken in the building, and a high degree of personalization goes into each Cadillac. Workers are allowed more time to do their respective jobs right.

Already the top luxury car on our market (sales were over 181,000 in 1965), Cadillacs are more refined this year. Technical improvements of major importance include a Saginaw-built variable-ratio power steering with 2.4 turns between locks. In normal road driving, there is a new preciseness of control and, as the wheel nears full lock, the ratio quickens, adding control in parking and accident-avoiding maneuvers. Steel strut-type autothermic pistons with slotted rail top rings are used for better oil control, a common problem with big-inch engines.

Rear brakes are all cast-iron, instead of composite iron and steel, for more uniform quality Effective lining area is greater too, and big 9.00 x 15-inch tubeless 2-ply tires are standard. They give better temperature control at high speeds and add seven miles per hour to the car's capabilities.

Now, let's look inside. In addition to 171 different interiors, from full perforated or unperforated leather to beautiful gold brocades, there are some very nice 1966 improvements.

Harold Warner is a hi-fi and stereo enthusiast, in addition to being general manager of Cadillac. So, it was no surprise to find one of the finest AM-FM stereo radios available in "his" car. Four speakers, arranged in "crossfire" fashion, are 180 degrees out of phase in every direction. It's like taking the Boston Philharmonic along to the corner drugstore.

Cadillac's new "hot seat" — they call it a seat warmer — shoots 150 watts of electricity through carbon yarn woven into pads under seats and seat backs of the front seats, giving instant heat when the key is turned on. This is tops for bottoms on those below-zero mornings, and it shuts off automatically when water temperature reaches 160°.

Cadillacs come in three passenger series, Calais, DeVille, and Fleetwood, plus the extra-luxurious limousines. Our test car was the middle-series DeVille four-door hardtop with a normal (for Cadillac owners) complement of accessories.

Our 3,000-mile road test covered all those states west of Detroit along famous Route 66. Weather varied from deluge to sunshine, from 35° to 100°, with day and night miles covered. We had an excellent chance to sample the luxuries of America's top-selling high-priced automobile and in the process, found out why there's an extra charge for first-class travel.

Comfort means many things to many people, and people with money come in as many different sizes and shapes as those without it. Cadillac's ride is pillowy soft, yet like a good pillow, is firm enough (a bit more so than the 1965 models) for good balance at cruising speeds. There's lots of stretch-out room inside and a huge trunk that'll hold all the suitcases any family should need.

"Adjustability" is big at Cadillac. Six-way power front seat, tilt-and-telescope steering wheel, full power (right down to the vent windows), Climate-Control, and Cruise-Control enable the driver to

Whisper-quiet at speed with good balance and control, car was an excellent tourer.

Adjustability of wheel, seats, speed, and temperature means top comfort on long trips.

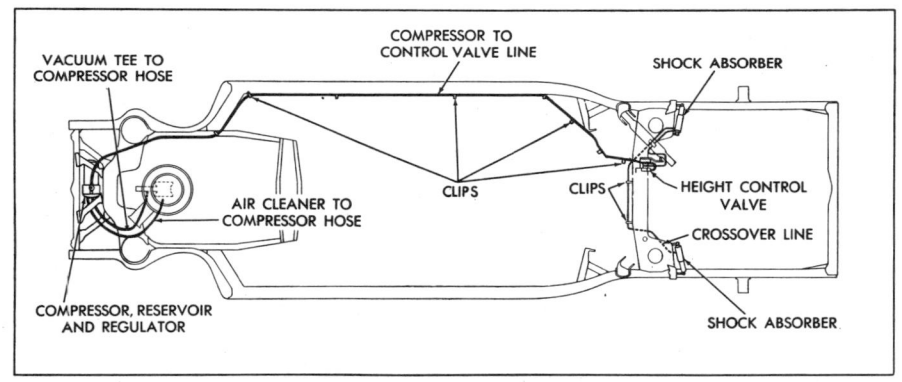

Despite passenger or trunk load, optional automatic load leveler keeps car level.

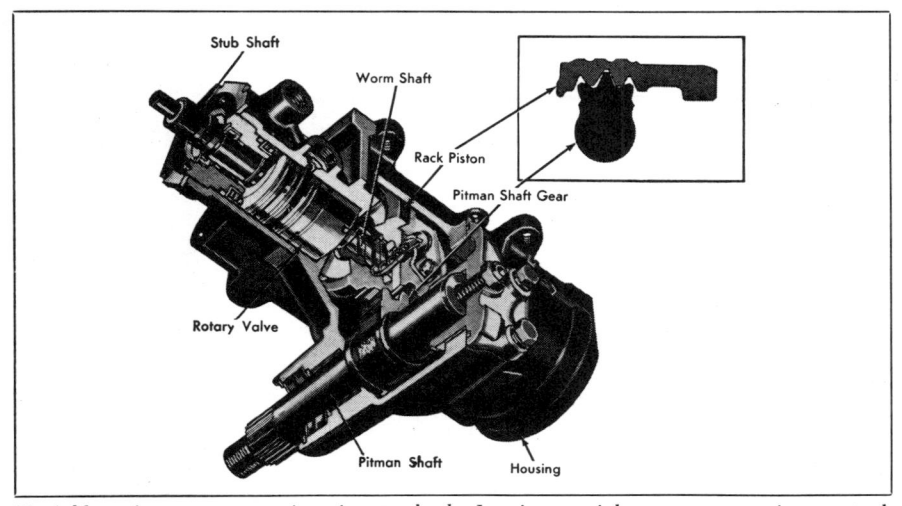

Variable-ratio power steering is standard. It gives quicker, more precise control.

"set it and forget it." In the wide-open areas, all we had to do was steer, try to keep the speedometer from nibbling at 80 and listen to stereo, of course. Mileage ranged from 13 to 14.5 mpg at highway speeds.

We found, too, that adjustability can have its drawbacks. We now understand why too many Cadillac owners settle down in air-conditioned isolation, aim their machines down the fast lane on a turnpike, and become oblivious to the presence of folks in lesser cars.

The "hot seat" should contain an automatic pin to remind one that the car really doesn't drive itself. The stereo should have another ear to pick up the horn blast of the fellow who wants to pass. The Cruise-Control should occasionally reach out and tickle the driver's foot. The automatic windows should lower at random to let in a bit of road noise. And, it should be mandatory that every Cadillac passenger have a grating voice and use it constantly. In essence, our complaint — or compliment, as you will — is that Cadillac has carried refinement to a degree that is soporific. /MT

More paint and less chrome make car look longer — but it's only an optical illusion.

CADILLAC

PHOTOS BY MC VAY, NORENBERG

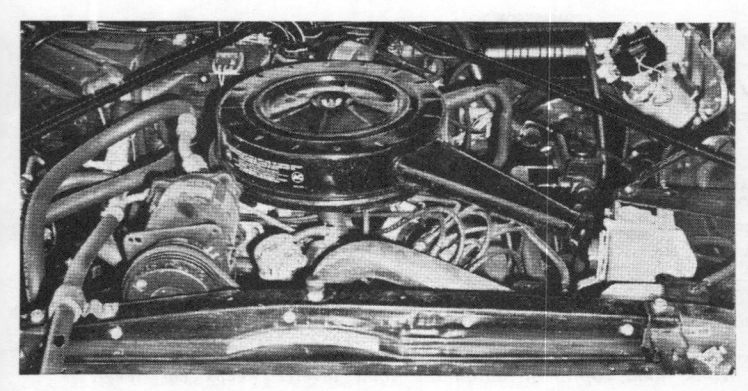

Tangle of accessories and connections is a mechanic's nightmare, but underneath it all lies a smooth, powerful, 429-inch V-8.

CADILLAC ACCESSORY PRICE LIST

Padded roof	$136.85
Leather upholstery	137.90
AM-FM stereo radio	287.90
6-way adjustable front seat	83.15
Climate-Control air conditioning	484.15
Tilt-and-telescope steering wheel	89.50
Power door locks (4 doors)	68.45
Twilight Sentinel	28.45
Remote-control trunk lock	52.10
Rear window defogger	26.35
Cruise-Control	94.75
Power vent windows	71.60
Closed crankcase vent system	50.00
Seat warmer (front only)	78.95
Bucket seats	184.20
Bucket seats with 4-way driver power, 2-way passenger power, 2 head rests, and reclining passenger seat back	321.04
Automatic level control	78.95
Controlled differential	52.65
Headrests (for bench seats)	52.65

CADILLAC SEDAN DE VILLE
4-door, 6-passenger hardtop

OPTIONS ON TEST CAR: Air conditioning, 6-way power seat, tilt/telescope steering wheel, power vents and door locks, AM-FM stereo radio, padded roof, leather upholstery, Twilight Sentinel, Cruise-Control, whitewalls, misc. access.
BASE PRICE: $5581
PRICE AS TESTED: $7306.25 (plus tax and license)
ODOMETER READING AT START OF TEST: 2723 miles
RECOMMENDED ENGINE RED LINE: 5000 rpm

PERFORMANCE

ACCELERATION (2 aboard)
0-30 mph.....3.5 secs.
0-45 mph.....6.8
0-60 mph.....11.1

PASSING TIMES AND DISTANCES
40-60 mph.....5.9 secs., 431 ft.
50-70 mph.....7.0 secs., 616 ft.

Standing start ¼-mile 17.7 secs. and 74 mph
Speeds in gears @ shift points
1st .....42 mph @ 4200 rpm   3rd .....100 mph @ 3700 rpm
2nd .....74 mph @ 4200 rpm

Speedometer Error on Test Car
| Car's speedometer reading | 31 | 46 | 52 | 63 | 75 | 86 |
| Weston electric speedometer | 30 | 45 | 50 | 60 | 70 | 80 |

Observed mph per 1000 rpm in top gear.....25 mph
Stopping Distances — from 30 mph, 35 ft.; from 60 mph, 170 ft.

SPECIFICATIONS FROM MANUFACTURER

Engine
Ohv V-8
Bore: 4.130 ins.
Stroke: 4.00 ins.
Displacement: 429 cu. ins.
Compression ratio: 10.5:1
Horsepower: 340 @ 4600 rpm
Horsepower per cubic inch: 0.79
Torque: 480 lbs.-ft. @ 3000 rpm
Carburetion: 1 4-bbl.
Ignition: 12-volt coil

Gearbox
3-speed automatic (Turbo Hydra-Matic); column-mounted lever

Driveshaft
1-piece, open tube

Differential
Hypoid, semi-floating
Ratio with air-conditioning: 3.21:1

Suspension
Front: Independent, with coil springs, upper A-arm, SLA with strut, tubular shocks, anti-roll bar
Rear: Rigid axle, coil springs, 4-link arms, tubular shocks

Steering
Variable-ratio ball nut sector with coaxial power assist
Turning diameter: 44.7 ft.
Turns lock to lock: 2.4

Wheels and Tires
15 x 6JK, 5-lug slotted steel disc wheels
9.00 x 15 tubeless, 2-ply (4-ply rated) tires

Brakes
Hydraulic, duo-servo, self-adjusting, with dual master cylinders
Front: 12-in. dia. x 2.5 ins. wide
Rear: 12-in. dia. x 2.5 ins. wide
Effective lining area: 221.8 sq. ins.
Swept drum area: 377.0 sq. ins.

Body and Frame
Separate steel body on perimeter frame
Wheelbase: 129.5 ins.
Track: front, 62.5 ins.; rear, 62.5 ins.
Overall length: 224.0 ins.
Overall width: 79.9 ins.
Overall height: 55.6 ins.
Curb weight: 4860 lbs.

Visit Your Authorized Cadillac Dealer

SOME OF OUR BEST FRIENDS ARE CHAUFFEURS. And there are a number of reasons why: the car's exceptional comfort, its great interior luxury, its new smoothness and quietness of operation, the marvelous ease provided by Cadillac's new steering and handling, and, of course, the car's impressive new stature and beauty. No wonder that wherever you find Cadillac chauffeurs—professional or amateur—you find a solid body of praise for the 1966 Cadillac, the world's most highly regarded luxury car. Drive it soon at your authorized dealer's. You'll discover why Cadillac makes friends so easily. *New elegance, new excellence, new excitement!*

| GM | Cadillac Motor Car Division

Cadillac 1966

Cadillac owners claim you get a lot to like

By BILL KILPATRICK,
PM's New York Automotive Editor

THE PAPER IS OLD, its edges yellowed and brittle to the touch. Yet the print is clear, the message as modern as a moonshot:

"Smooth-riding, powerful, absolutely dependable, the Cadillac is a car surprising alike in performance and cost."

This quote from a 1904 advertisement for the car that once billed itself as the "standard of the world" accurately summarizes the opinions of most 1966 Cadillac owners surveyed by PM. Even as the copywriter of over 60 years ago claimed, Cadillac owners still find today's car "smooth-riding, powerful...dependable" and they like its performance.

But many owners—based on what they feel they got for their money—think "surprising" is hardly the word to describe the $5000-plus cost of the car.

"It's time the makers of all cars start producing a car worth what they ask for it," wrote an Illinois businessman.

A Massachusetts claims investigator, however, said of her 1966 two-door Cadillac, "It's an excellent car from the front to rear bumper and in my opinion has no equal."

What has no equal, owners surveyed by PM feel, is the way the car handles, an attribute to which they accorded an FMR (frequency-of-mention rating) of 36.8 percent. Next in order, Cadillac owners praised comfort (34.4 percent), ride (29.4 percent) and styling (22.7 percent).

But owning a new Cadillac apparently isn't all roses, either. Even owners generally pleased with their cars added to the complaints listed by those who regard their comparatively expensive investments as a waste of money.

Owners didn't like, for example, wind noise, a gripe to which they accorded an FMR of 9.8 percent. Also at this rating level were complaints of various rattles and noises, hardly the sort of thing one expects from the "standard of the world." Tied with FMRs of 8.9 percent were assorted knocks about Cadillac's automatic climate control airconditioning and heater system (it either doesn't work or it works too well) and overall workmanship. Most emphatic, despite an FMR of only 7.3 percent, were owner complaints about location and size of the glove compartment. All by itself, surprisingly, was an old

The affluent folk like:

Handling 36.8%
Comfort 34.4
Ride 29.4

But don't like:

Wind noise 9.8%
Rattles/noise 9.8
Climate control system 8.9

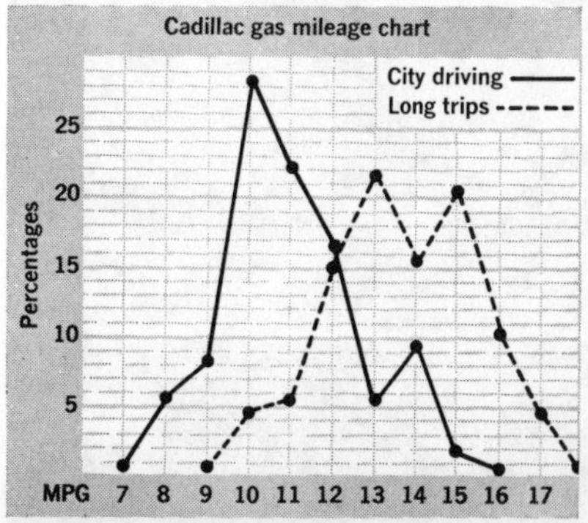

CADILLAC AND THRIFT aren't synonymous, owners say. Engine is 429-cubic-incher, puts out big 340 hp

AWKWARD AND SMALL glove compartment drew owner ire. Contents tend to spill when it's opened

CADILLAC PARKS EASILY, many owners claim, citing handling as a big plus. Power steering is standard

CADILLAC OWNERS' REPORT

Michigan engineer feels: "Overall style is far ahead of other so-called luxury cars."

"I appreciate the simple, uncluttered lines and lack of gingerbread."—Florida engineer.

"Tops for beauty and luxury, inside and out."—Virginia salesman.

Another thing Cadillac owners feel they obtain with their bill-of-sale is reliability.

"I have found the Cadillac to be the most dependable car I have ever owned."—New Mexico, retired.

"I can drive it a full year with little or no service."—New York optometrist.

"Car offers good all-'round dependability."—New Jersey technician.

Despite the positive note struck by owner praises, however, America's Motoring Majesty has some loyal (generally) opposition, most of it like communists in the French Assembly—small in percentage, but loud.

"There's a lot of noise around the windows and door frames."—District of Columbia showman.

"We have a wind whistle with our '66 that we didn't have with our '64."—South Dakota housewife.

"I get a lot of noise through and around the front windows."—Wisconsin educator.

Added to wind noise are complaints about rattles and road noise.

"It rattles like a truck."—Michigan broker.

"Body isn't as tight as in previous Cadillacs I've owned."—California executive.

"Rumbling noise from the road seems to come right up into the car."—New Hampshire clergyman.

In theory the automatic climate control system sounds peachy, but in practice a number of owners think it's a dud, or at least something less than its billing.

"The climate control does not operate fully automatically, as the salesman said it did. I think the thermostat is too sensitive and the warm air suddenly changes to cold before a comfortable temperature is reached."—Connecticut physician.

▶ **I found this to be true in PM's test car, too.**

"It's hard to control the heater part of the climate control."—Michigan engineer.

Next on the complaint list is a category one hardly expects to find when it comes to a Cadillac: workmanship. As pointed out in previous owners reports, poor and/or indifferent workmanship seemingly dogs the entire auto industry. Still, with the "little" Caddy selling for just under $5000, it's more than out of place, particularly with the "standard of the world." A Maryland businessman makes the point:

"A car in this price field shouldn't have as many faults in workmanship as does mine. For example, there were several loose bolts, the rubber window molding was twisted, and so on. The car has several signs of negligent workmanship."

"More attention should be paid to small details of workmanship. There were loose thread ends hanging all over my new car's upholstery."—New Jersey businessman.

"The doors have never fit properly and the rear speaker rattles."—Virginia executive.

"They ought to do a better job of assembly. With my last ten Cadillacs it has taken me almost 7000 miles to get all the bugs out."—Florida, retired.

▶ **This is no fair-weather friend, either. He has owned 32 Cadillacs.**

Owners aren't too happy with the glove compartment. It's a minor item, granted, but one would think that in a Cadillac it would be both copious and efficient.

"It's awkward."—Michigan doctor.

"It's too small!"—Iowa sales manager.

"Things tumble out when its opened."—California contractor.

"It's next to useless."—Maryland executive.

And so on, all pretty much in the same vein. So are comments about the front seat ashtray.

"It's unhandy."—Florida businessman.

"Inconvenient."—Michigan physician.

"Too small."—California businessman.

"The ashtrays up front are just terrible."—Illinois accountant.

Ranked sixth on the praise list by Cadillac owners was the car's quietness; again, something one would think comes with possession of the ignition key.

"The engine is very quiet."—Iowa executive.

"Car just whispers along at high speeds."—Pennsylvania designer.

"Road noise is minimal."—Tennessee sales executive.

Many owners had kind words for their cars' pickup and performance.

"Best performing car yet."—Kentucky businessman.

"Responds well when I step on the gas."—Virginia manager.

"Acceleration characteristics are superb."—Ohio supervisor.

Although, as mentioned earlier, many owners deemed the climate control system bad news.

---

lament traditionally expressed by Cadillac owners. An Iowa sales executive wrote, "My biggest complaint is that just because you drive a Cadillac, motels, garages, gas stations and any other place of service will try to take you. Why, just this year a (brand) station tried to tell me I needed new shocks when I had only 5000 miles on my car."

So, accolades aside, realize that wearing a Cadillac crown apparently can be a heavy, expensive responsibility at times. Cadillac owners responding to PM's survey rolled up an aggregate of 1,011,746 miles of both around-town and long-trip driving during which they averaged overall 12.4 mpg. But discussing Cadillacs and mileage is like J.P. Morgan's commentary on yachting—if you're concerned about cost, you can't afford it. Anyway, here's what the surveyed owners of 1966 Cadillacs had to say for and against. Their comments are listed in order of frequency mentioned. The boldface comments are the author's.

"I like the way the car drives and handles. It's smooth, quiet, and I like the secure feeling of driving a car such as a Cadillac."—Michigan engineer.

"Very easy to handle during parking."—Indiana, retired.

"It's solid, quick steering and precise."—Massachusetts druggist.

"Although it's a large, heavy car, it handles well."—California supervisor.

Next on the praise list was plain ol' down-home comfort, an undeniable attribute of just about any Cadillac extant. That people often buy a certain car for a specific reason is verified by a Nebraska attorney, who wrote:

"I bought my Cadillac because it was the most comfortable car I could buy."

"Extremely smooth to ride in and tireless on long trips."—Iowa, retired.

"We find our Cadillac spacious, with ample, luxurious room for others."—Ohio housewife.

Listed almost on a par with comfort was ride.

"Excellent ride. No tendency to bottom-out when going over dips in the road."—Michigan tool engineer.

"The car has outstanding riding qualities in both city and mountain driving."—California, retired.

"It's like a cruiser going over small swells in the ocean."—Missouri contractor.

▶ **In Missouri?**

One thing most Cadillac owners feel they get for their money is one of the best looking cars on the road. Part of this, I'm sure, stems from the car's prestige mystique—at these prices it *better* be good looking. Actually, however, from a styling point of view, Cadillacs aren't too different from similar Detroit products. Yet a

---

Summary of Cadillac Owners' Reports

Excellent ... 67.2%   Good ... 26.8%   Fair ... 4.4%   Poor ... 1.6%

Best-liked features:	
Handling	36.8%
Comfort	34.4
Ride	29.4
Styling	22.7
Reliability	14.1
Quietness	12.3
Performance	9.8
Climate control	9.2
Roadability	8.0
Workmanship	6.1
Least-liked features:	
Wind noise	9.8
Rattles/noise	9.8
Climate control	8.9
Workmanship	8.9
Glove compartment	7.3
Ashtrays	7.3
Finish/paint	7.3
Gasoline consumption	6.5
Styling	5.7
Window glass/lack of molding	5.7
Most liked to see changed:	
Glove compartment (size/position)	11.9
Styling	10.4
Ashtrays, lighters (more)	9.0
Better climate control	7.5
Headroom	6.7
Steering wheel position/size	3.7
Instrument panel/dash	3.7
Better fuel economy	3.7
Price (lower it)	3.0
Car traded in:	
Cadillac	77.8
Oldsmobile	8.1
Pontiac	3.4
Buick	3.4
Thunderbird	3.4
Mercury	1.3
Others	2.0
Dealer service:	
Excellent	61.9
Average	31.3
Poor	6.8
Buy from dealer again?	
Yes	91.5
No	8.5
Buy another Cadillac?	
Yes	98.1
No	1.9
Bought Cadillac because:	
Value/trade-in	38.5
Past experience	21.2
Styling	13.5%
Prestige	11.5
Comfort	9.6
Availability	7.7
Different (something new)	5.8
Dealer/dealer service	5.8
Considered other makes?	
No	68.7
Yes	31.3
Own another car?	
No	68.3
Yes	31.7
Make of other car:	
Chevrolet	28.1
Ford	16.5
Pontiac	14.0
Buick	12.4
Oldsmobile	9.9
Cadillac (another one)	7.4
Thunderbird	5.0
Mustang	5.0
Corvair	4.1
Dodge	3.3
Volkswagen	2.5
Mercury	1.7
Others	14.9
Total miles driven:	1,011,746

CADILLAC FOR 1967
Refinement of Elegance

CADILLAC COUPE DE VILLE shows new exterior styling for '67. Sculpture line extends from headlights to taillights.

FLEETWOOD BROUGHAM continues on 133-in. wheelbase, has 429-cu. in. V-8 for power and Turbo Hydra-Matic transmission as standard.

DE VILLE convertible offers high-style luxury in contemporary good taste. Seatback headrests are a new-for-Cadillac option.

ALONG WITH its outstanding new personal car, Eldorado, Cadillac Division of General Motors has produced refinements on its regular lines for the 1967 model year. Safety items, of course, will receive the most public attention, but engineering and styling changes are important, too.

Engine improvements include a new production-line cylinder bore finishing technique and new rings for better immediate oil economy, and the specification of Quadrajet 4-barrel carburetors for all Cadillacs. Laminated mylar printed circuits serve the instrument panel. A new fan clutch and modified body mounts give significantly quieter operation.

Model lineup among the '67 Cadillacs is virtually identical to '66; the former Eldorado convertible, however, has been replaced by the front-drive Eldorado (see Page 44). Twelve body styles in three series are offered. Calais and De Ville share 129.5-in. wheelbases, Fleetwood has a 133-in. wheelbase and the Seventy-Five sedan and limousine have a 149.8-in. wheelbase. The Eldorado, which is classed with the Fleetwood series, has a 120-in. wheelbase. Styling changes reflect the traditional Cadillac elements of cross-hatched grille and sharply peaked fender lines. A side-panel design line sweeps fore to aft, curving downward to the rear. Taillights, stoplights and backup lights are all integrated into vertical rear bumper elements.

DE-FOGGER for rear windows is a new-for-'67 Cadillac feature.

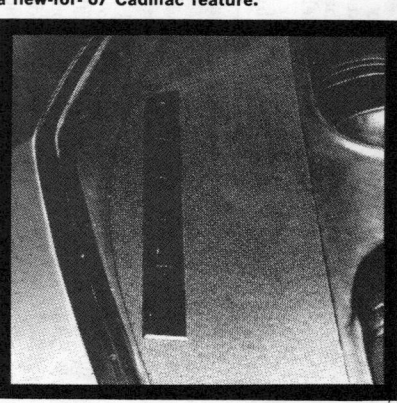

MINI-TESTS *C/D presents a guide to the 1968 American cars*

Cadillac Fleetwood Eldorado

The Cadillac Eldorado, a high-roller's version of the Oldsmobile Toronado, is a front-wheel-drive vehicle powered by the world's largest passenger car engine, which, by all that's theoretically holy, ought to be an unmanageable handful. Actually, it's very controllable at turnpike speeds, particularly in transient response (a high-speed slalom to test evasive maneuverability).

Whether or not the Eldorado is worth the $1850 or so above the cost of the Toronado depends on such intangibles as status and an appreciation of the Cadillac's higher-quality materials and better quality control. As for luxury, comfort and space for the driver and front-seat passenger are as good as the bigger Cadillacs.

Last year we were very critical of the Eldorado's standard drum brakes, particularly their lack of directional stability in a high-speed panic stop. Cadillac has now made front disc brakes standard.

Performance is good, but almost unfelt. Despite the presence of almost eight liters of V-8 towing the Eldorado along, the engine is tuned for smoothness and silence.

We like the Eldorado's appearance; it's probably the most understated expression of taste Cadillac has ever exhibited. It's sleek, clean, and it looks expensive—which is half the fun of getting there.

CADILLAC FLEETWOOD ELDORADO	
Manufacturer:	Cadillac Division, General Motors Corporation, Detroit, Michigan
CAR AS TESTED	
Engine	375-hp, 472 cu. in. V-8
Transmission	3-speed automatic
Steering	Power-assisted
Suspension	Standard
Brakes	Disc F, Drum R

CHECK LIST

ENGINE	
Throttle Response	Good
Noise Insulation	Excellent
DRIVE TRAIN	
Shift Linkage	Very Good
Shift Smoothness	Excellent
STEERING	
Effort	Very Good
Response	Very Good
HANDLING	
Predictability	Very Good
Evasive Maneuverability	Good
BRAKES	
Directional Stability	Good
Fade Resistance	Good
INTERIOR	
Ease of Entry/Exit	Very Good
Driving Position	Very Good
Front Seating Comfort	Very Good
Rear Seating Comfort	Fair
GENERAL	
Vision	Fair
Heater/Defroster	Excellent
Weather Sealing	Excellent
Trunk Space	Good

Cadillac Coupe de Ville

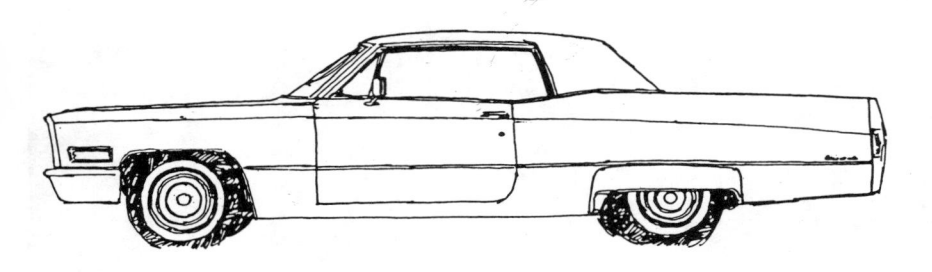

Surprising as it may seem, the Cadillac Coupe de Ville is a pretty fair driver's car. Getting the most out of a car's over-the-road performance depends to a large degree on the driver's ability to get comfortable at the wheel. The Coupe's 6-way power seat and tilting/telescoping steering wheel options make it posssible to arrange the driving position to suit Junior Johnson or Stirling Moss or anybody in between.

The suspension is soft—too soft—but it responds well to the controls. A set of Koni shock absorbers would probably eliminate our few objections to its ride and handling characteristics. Cadillacs are equipped with very large tires, and while they develop a good bite in high-speed turns, at low speeds the car plows alarmingly if driven hard. Thanks to a variable ratio gear in the power steering system, the Coupe de Ville is very responsive to steering inputs.

Despite the Coupe de Ville's bigger-than-life dimensions (129.5-in. wheelbase, 224.7-in. overall length—bigger in both respects than a Chrysler *station wagon*), it really is a *coupe,* and rear seat passengers are a little cramped. Nevertheless we like the Coupe de Ville's appearance—a little too massive to be actually called beautiful, but infused with a subtle tastefulness that is appealing and has made Cadillac the most prestigious car built in this country.

CADILLAC COUPE DE VILLE	
Manufacturer:	Cadillac Motor Division, General Motors Corporation, Detroit, Michigan
Engine	375-hp, 472 cu. in. V-8
Transmission	3-speed automatic
Steering	Power-assisted
Suspension	Standard
Brakes	Drum F, Drum R

CHECK LIST

ENGINE	
Throttle Response	Very Good
Noise Insulation	Excellent
DRIVE TRAIN	
Shift Linkage	Very Good
Shift Smoothness	Very Good
STEERING	
Effort	Excellent
Response	Good
HANDLING	
Predictability	Very Good
Evasive Maneuverability	Good
BRAKES	
Directional Stability	Very Good
Fade Resistance	Good
INTERIOR	
Ease of Entry/Exit	Very Good
Driving Position	Excellent
Front Seating Comfort	Excellent
Rear Seating Comfort	Good
GENERAL	
Vision	Good
Heater/Defroster	Excellent
Weather Sealing	Excellent
Trunk Space	Very Good

Arrival of the Fittest

By Bill Sanders

Yes! We have arrived, haven't we. A gossamer web of material wealth: every man's dream. We've reached the culmination of that lofty, sublime zenith known as "having it made." The house and pool in Trousdale. Or maybe it's a mansion in Pacific Heights or a penthouse apartment high above Sutton Place. We've just purchased an early Seurat for the den. And now it's time. Time for that new automobile. • The ad men know where it's at. As we glance through *The New Yorker*, *Holiday*, even *Life*, we find them there, the Cads, Continentals and Imperials . . . parked in front of The Fairmont or The St. Moritz, a genesis of Pierre Cardin dinner jackets, Lord & Taylor evening gowns and the ubiquitous glitter of authentic Tiffany ice. • Sure, you want comfort, luxury, all the solid dependability a car in this class should have. But come on, man, let's drop the pretenses. Let's have a little honesty. See the doorman in those ads? Well, that's where it's really at. After we're through with all the justifications in the guise of mechanical and comfort reasoning we get down to basics. This car should be, and is, a symbol. Like those other acquisitions, a symbol of our predominence in the eyes of our peers. Yes, folks, our American nemesis . . . the Status Symbol. Top of the line status symbol. We pay homage to ostentation; it's part of our condition if you're adroit enough to maintain the image. As Dumas said: "Nothing succeeds like success." • We have our thesis; comparison is now legitimate. Coupe de Ville, Continental, Imperial; which gives the most status? Where do you go for a valid reaction? The doorman, the parking attendants. Manhattan, Miami, Chicago, San Francisco, Beverly Hills . . . at the clubs, the restaurants; which cars materialize first? Which are parked back there in the corner or out in front? That's the gauntlet they have to run. *The* Test. Status. That's the clincher. But before the *raison d'etre*, let's compare some of the tangible benefits you ascribe to for almost eight grand.

Even the names conjure up visions of aristocratic splendor: Imperial Le Baron, Coupe de Ville, Continental.

COMFORT & RIDE

Some divergence in seating comfort is evident, but only in degree. Full creature comfort is the goal in each car, consequently everything is supple, thickly padded and plush. Our Imperial had individual bucket seats; the Cadillac and Lincoln-Continental had bench-type seats with bucket backs and folding center armrests. The Imperial also had a folding center armrest, which, when up made the central part of the front seats available for a third passenger. Bucket seats in the Imperial were comfortable and front seat leg room was spacious. Having each seat individually adjustable is a desirable feature. The Continental seats were the most comfortable from every consideration of all three cars. As we stated, though, this is only by a slight degree. Continental seatbacks are effectively contoured to hold you firmly, besides being deeply padded. Huge Coupe de Ville seats *look* great with their space-age design headrests, and comfort matches looks.

Six-way power seat adjustments are a must for cars of this calibre. They aid driving and riding comfort immeasurably. In a group of cars all weighing close to 5000 pounds with suspensions designed to give the smoothest, softest boulevard ride, each has come comparatively close to maximum potential.

Rear seat room and luxuriousness is much more divergent. Considering the size of these cars, more rear seat room could be allocated, but both the Cadillac and Continental had adequate leg room. In fact, the de Ville had enough leg room to move around comfortably. Rear seating in the Cadillac Coupe de Ville is deliciously intimate and private.

Imperial rear seat leg room was dismally inadequate. With bucket seats in a full rearward position there was absolutely no knee room on the right side. A good feature on the Imperial is an automatic front seat adjuster. Push the back forward on the right hand bucket seat to enter or leave the rear seat and the power-operated bucket seat moves forward automatically to the most forward position, allowing an easy step in or out.

Rear seat headroom was good in each car despite the low overall height.

CONVENIENCE & UTILITY

Each car has power window and door locks placed in armrests, convenient for driver and passengers. Lighters and ashtrays are placed close to each passenger location. Inside door

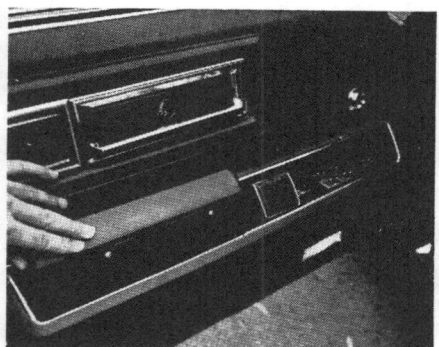

Imperial LeBaron

(Above, left to right) Imperial has a small red light just above the window and door lock switches in driver's door to make it easier to locate the right switch at night. Entire instrument panel is illuminated rather than individual instruments, causing too much reflection. For a large car, the Imperial has very little leg room, though a good feature is the automatic front adjuster on the two-door. When the right hand seatback is pushed forward for entry or exit of the rear seat, the seat moves forward automatically to its front position. (Right and below) New styling is very tasteful and contemporary.

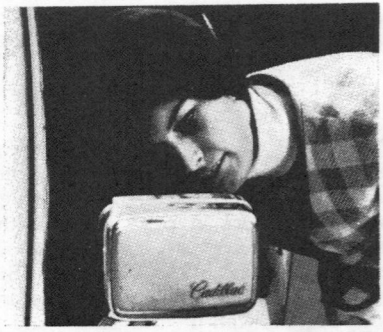

Photos by: Pat Brollier, Gerry Stiles, George Foon, Dan Schimmel

Arrival of the Fittest

handles are most convenient and easy to operate on the Imperial. The Lincoln rates second. You almost have to get a new wrist to open the Cadillac doors from inside. A continuous shelf still runs across the top of the Imperial dash, with instruments and switches located on a flat panel beneath. Both the Lincoln and Cadillac have instrument panels recessed in front of the driver with a padded ridge projecting out and around. Complete instrumentation is a good feature of the Imperial dash. The other two use only a fuel gauge. Chrysler uses a new "floodlight" effect for instrument illumination. Light shines down on the entire dash rather than coming from the instruments as in normal use. We don't like this new approach. There is too much reflection from the gauges. Chrysler has also incorporated a small red light just above the window and door lock switches in the driver's door, making it easier to locate the correct switch while driving at night.

We like the instrument panel layout on the Coupe de Ville and Continental, except for the fact that instruments and switches are only visible and accessible by the driver. Door armrests that conceal storage boxes are a great convenience item on the Imperial.

Each car has a cruise control. Cadillac still has it on the dash with a revolving drum for speed selection. We like the type used by the Continental and Imperial better. A simple button is located in the turn lever indicator. We can't understand why Lincoln doesn't use the same cruise control setup as the Thunderbird, which is far and away the best of any car, with buttons located in the center bar of the steering wheel.

Each car has a huge, carpeted trunk. The Lincoln has the most meticulously appointed luggage area, with the spare and jack also covered by carpeting.

HANDLING & STEERING

For the price you pay, the Imperial has one big thing going for it. Unfortunately, not many luxury car owners will be interested in peerless handling characteristics. Even on the road course at Orange County Raceway, the Imperial was edifying when it came to handling. In fact, it handles as well as cars half its size. It goes into corners as hard as you care to push it and drifts effortlessly with only minor understeer. And, the Imperial is more than five inches longer than in 1968.

As we said earlier, ride is ideal for ponderous cars, but both the Cad and Lincoln handle like what they are; ponderous cars. Taking a sharp turn too fast in the Lincoln is quite an experience. First you feel the outside tire start to roll under as the car plows. Next, the sensation is felt that the wheel too will go under if you don't slow down. So you'd better back off.

Variable ratio steering is a good feature on the Cad, but under conditions of hard handling the front end and steering felt wobbly, which was probably due to the quickly changing ratio; we never experienced it at any other

Cadillac Coupe de Ville

(Opposite bottom, left to right) Dials are not as complete as one who is interested in "how his car is running" might desire, but what is there is easy to read. All are recessed in a padded compartment in front of the driver, but perimeter projections appear as though they could be absolutely dangerous for a center passenger in case of a collision. Rear seat room and comfort in the two-door de Ville is surprisingly better than four-door competitors. The Lincoln may have the most meticulously appointed trunk, but the Cadillac Coupe de Ville's sure one helluva gas.

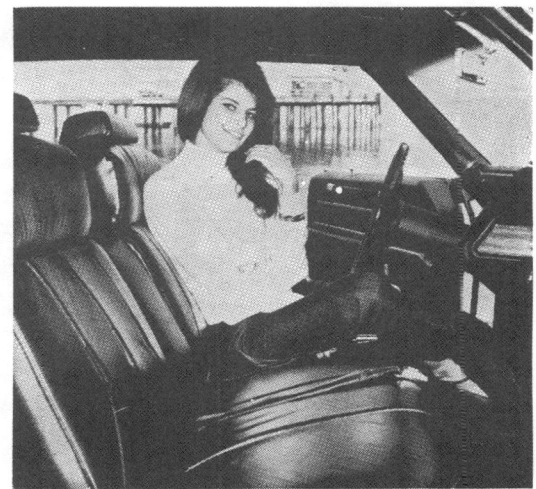

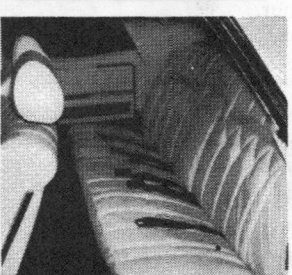

Lincoln Continental

(Far left) For years we've been carping about the dreadful brakes on domestics, so you can imagine our awe when the Continental stopped from 60 mph in less than 110 feet. (Left) Rear seat room is adequate, but should be better in four-door. Quality was best of all cars. (Left corner) New grille received criticism as resembling mid-Fifties bug screen. Door contains all power controls in very easy-to-find and functional arrangement. Trunk is pure class.

Arrival of the Fittest

time. Understeer was also very noticeable on the Cad, although it didn't have the desperate roll and pitch of the Continental in really hard corners.

BRAKING

We know the stopping distances of the Imperial and Continental from 60 mph will cause an avalanche of letters, but the distances [Imperial: 116.7 feet, Continental: 109.9 feet] represent the mean and are not even the *best* of the multiple stops made.

Our test Imperial showed a 100 percent improvement over the 1968 model we tested. Stopping from 60 mph our Continental experienced considerable rear wheel hop. While it didn't affect stability, the wheel hop was uncomfortable.

Stopping in what must be considered a more "normal" distance from

PERFORMANCE

	CHRYSLER IMPERIAL LE BARON	LINCOLN CONTINENTAL	CADILLAC COUPE DE VILLE
Acceleration			
0-30 mph	4.3 secs.	3.3 secs.	3.5 secs.
0-45 mph	7.3 secs.	5.6 secs.	5.8 secs.
0-60 mph	11.6 secs.	9.0 secs.	9.4 secs.
0-75 mph	18.4 secs.	13.3 secs.	13.9 secs.
Standing Start ¼-Mile	82.1 mph 17.2 secs.	85.7 mph 16.2 secs.	83.8 mph 16.5 secs.
Passing Speeds			
40-60 mph	7.0 secs. 512.4 ft.	5.0 secs. 366.0 ft.	4.9 secs. 358.6 ft.
50-70 mph	7.4 secs. 651.2 ft.	5.1 secs. 448.8 ft.	5.6 secs. 492.8 ft.
Speeds in Gears			
1st ...mph @ rpm	51 @ 4400	53 @ 4600	52 @ 4400
2nd ...mph @ rpm	86 @ 4400	88 @ 4600	85 @ 4400
3rd ...mph @ rpm	84 @ 3000	95 @ 3500	98 @ 3500
MPH per 1000 rpm (in top gear)	28.0 mph	27.1 mph	28.0 mph
Stopping Distances			
From 30 mph	19.0 ft.	29.0 ft.	26.2 ft.
From 60 mph	116.7 ft.	109.9 ft.	149.8 ft.
Gas Mileage Range	9.0 to 10.8 mpg	8.6 to 10.0 mpg	9.2 to 11.8 mpg

Arrival of the Fittest

60 mph, the Cadillac experienced a definite lack of stability and required much more wheel correction.

PERFORMANCE

If our thesis of status holds true we are sure prospective investors won't develop ulcers at the thought of quarter-mile times for these cars. However, they do perform adequately for their power-to-weight ratios and have adequate push for passing situations. In the performance race, the lively Continental beat the Coupe de Ville, even though the latter has ten more horsepower and 25 more lbs.-ft. torque.

QUALITY & CONSTRUCTION

This evaluation is probably the most important, even considering status and prestige. Examining all the salient features, such as quiet ride, solid construction, quality of workmanship and materials, we've got to give it to the Continental. Even the vaunted Cadillac has lost some of its quality aspects from 1968. The Continental evidences a much closer attention to detail in construction and has the quietest ride. Both the Cadillac and Imperial seem to utilize too much plastic and flimsy material where it shouldn't be used or seen. One feature mars the Lincoln. The automatic headlight dimmer switch is on the left front fender in a position that detracts from the car's appearance. The other cars have it hidden behind the grille.

The lack of quality in our Imperial was annoying. With only several thousand miles on the odometer, rattles were already developing. Overall finish was not up to that of the other two tested.

STATUS

Back to the beginning. Status. Prestige. After all is said and done, where it's truly at. What does make the heads turn and the doormen and parking attendants hustle just a little faster in deference to what you're driving? Since Beverly Hills is our closest laboratory, we experimented there. Result in the Status Standings: the Coupe de Ville is still king, with the Continental a close second and the newly styled Imperial a grudging third.

Unfortunately our Continental was a light bronze color with a white vinyl top, a definite detraction. All black. That's the only route for a four-door Continental. And for that reason and the overall quality we have to go the whole route with Lincoln.

/MT

SPECIFICATIONS

	CHRYSLER IMPERIAL LE BARON	LINCOLN CONTINENTAL	CADILLAC COUPE DE VILLE
Engine:	90° OHV V-8	90° OHV V-8	90° OHV V-8
Bore & Stroke — ins.	4.32 x 3.75	4.36 x 3.85	4.30 x 4.06
Displacement — cu. in.	440	460	472
HP @ RPM	350 @ 4400	365 @ 4600	375 @ 4400
Torque: lbs.-ft. @ rpm	480 @ 2800	500 @ 2800	525 @ 3000
Compression Ratio	10.1:1	10.5:1	10.5:1
Carburetion	1 4-bbl.	1 4-bbl.	1 4-bbl.
Transmission	automatic	automatic	automatic
Final Drive Ratio	2.94:1	3.00:1	2.94:1
Steering Type	Power	Power	Variable Ratio Power
Steering Ratio	19.08:1	20.4:1	12.2:1 — 16.0:1
Turning Diameter (Curb-to-curb-ft.)	44.9	46.7	44.8
Wheel Turns (lock-to-lock)	3.5	3.3	3.1
Tire Size	9.15 x 15	9.15 x 15	9.00 x 15
Brakes	Power front disc, drum rear	Power front disc, drum rear	Power front disc, drum rear
Front Suspension	Independent torsion bar	Independent coil springs	Independent coil springs
Rear Suspension	Semi-elliptic multi leaf	Semi-elliptic multi leaf	Trailing arm, coil springs
Body/Frame Construction	Unitized	Unitized	Separate Body/Frame
Wheelbase — ins.	127.0	126.0	129.5
Overall Length — ins.	229.7	224.2	225.0
Width — ins.	79.2	79.7	79.8
Height — ins.	55.1	54.9	54.4
Front Track — ins.	62.4	62.4	62.5
Rear Track — ins.	61.1	61.0	62.5
Curb Weight — lbs.	4980	5208	4780
Fuel Capacity — gals.	24	25.5	26
Oil Capacity — qts.	4	4	4

PRICES/OPTIONS

IMPERIAL LE BARON

2-door hardtop base price	$5788.00
Imperial Le Baron Bucket seats — leather — dark saddle	361.60
Sure Grip differential	58.00
Tinted glass	54.25
Air conditioning/heater/automatic temperature	507.85
Door edge protectors	5.20
License plate frame — front and rear	12.10
Automatic speed control	85.35
Power seat — bucket — 6 way — left & right	217.10
Power door locks	47.90
Power trunk lid release	30.50
Radio — Golden Touch Tuner — AM/FM: Includes rear seat speaker and power antenna	234.35
Steering wheel tilt and telescope	95.20
Fiber glass belt tires 9.15x15	83.45

LINCOLN CONTINENTAL

Lincoln Continental 4-door sedan base price	$6063.00
Leather with vinyl interior	137.80
White vinyl roof	152.20
9.15x15 Belted Tires	56.40
Power vent windows	72.20
6-way power seat with passenger recliner	149.60
Spare tire cover	11.90
Tilt steering wheel	72.20
Deck lid release and speed control	135.20
Rear window defogger with environment control	42.00
Air conditioner	503.70
AM/FM radio, rear speaker, power antenna	244.00
Automatic headlamp dimmer	51.20
Tinted glass	52.50
Appearance protection group	18.40
Power door locks	68.20
Flared wheel covers	59.10
Automatic ride control	97.10

CADILLAC COUPE DE VILLE

Cadillac Coupe de Ville base price	$5720.90
Vinyl roof	152.65
Leather upholstery	137.90
Twin rubber floor mats front & rear	16.70
Five white wall tires	56.85
Stereo radio (AM/FM)	288.40
Soft-ray glass	52.65
6-way front seat adjuster	89.50
Two door edge guards	5.30
Automatic climate control	515.75
Power door locks & seatback release	68.45
Tilt & telescope steering wheel	94.75
Twilight sentinel	31.60
Remote-control trunk lock	52.65
Rear window de-fogger	26.35
Cruise control	94.75
Guide-matic headlamp control	50.55

A car with an image like the Cadillac's cannot afford to look ordinary or cluttered. The design is simple but impressive.

SNOB APPEAL ON WHEELS

The Cadillac Coupe De Ville. Take an easy chair from here to there.

There are any number of super-luxury cars on the American market today — all of them with plenty to offer in the field of comfort, style and prestige. But the name that almost invariably springs to mind when the average American thinks of luxury automobiles is that most regal of the General Motors hierarchy, the Cadillac.

The Cadillac is even more of a symbol of American opulence in the minds of non-Americans. To them, this is the *ultimate* American automobile. The Cadillac has built itself such a reputation for luxurious living on wheels that the very name has become a symbol of prestige. The Cadillac is to America what the Rolls Royce is to Mother England ... though in a flamboyant, ostentatious and typically American manner.

Not that a car like the Cadillac Coupe De Ville would be everyone's choice, however. For every thousand motorists who would drool and slaver at the thought of owning the golden giant that is the subject of this test, there are certainly a thousand more who would wrinkle their noses and shudder at the thought of even driving such a huge display of vulgar wealth.

Generally, you either love the Cadillac image or hate it with a passion. There are very few people with 'in-between' feelings about it.

Power train

So what does the Coupe De Ville have to offer? First of all there is the fact that just about everything that can be automatic, *is*. Then consider that practically every 'extra' listed for normal automobiles comes as standard on the Coupe De Ville and you see the reason why it needs the largest passenger car engine known to man to lug the whole package around.

Introduced in 1968, the massive V8 has a displacement of no less than 472 cubic inches. It is easily the largest passenger car engine in regular production anywhere in the world.

Despite the monstrous displacement figure, however, the Cadillac engine is not a super-powerful one. Its horsepower figure is a conservative 375 and it is certain that less than half of that finds its way through the innumerable accessory drives and the drag of the automatic transmission and out on to the rear wheels.

Where the thing does score is in terms of torque. At a mere 3000rpm it develops a staggering 525 lb/ft of torque, a figure unsurpassed by any other passenger car engine.

The unit's eight cylinders are set in the usual vee-formation with an angle of 90 degrees between each bank of four.

Bore and stroke are 4.30 inches by 4.06 inches respectively and it is a slow-revving engine with maximum brake horsepower being developed at only 4,400rpm.

The cooling system is sealed and the only time that the radiator cap should be removed (unless something untoward happens and you lose all your coolant) is to change the cooling fluid once every two years.

As the system is pressurized between 13.5 to 16.5 lb. per square inch, you are certain to get a shower of extremely hot liquid if you remove the radiator cap after the engine has been running for some time.

Coolant level can be checked in the transparent reservoir to the right of the radiator and extra coolant added *to the reservoir,* if necessary and when the engine is cool.

The cooling system contains 21.3 U.S. quarts of coolant or 21.8 if the car is fitted with air-conditioning. The system is controlled by a thermostat which begins to open at around 192 degrees Fahrenheit and is fully open at 217 degrees.

The sump, including the oil filter, holds four quarts of oil and the automatic transmission looks after a further four. Another five pints are contained in the rear axle.

Standard transmission on the Coupe De Ville is the well-proven and well-liked Turbo Hydramatic, one of the best-ever American automatic transmissions.

It has three forward gears on the selector quadrant plus the usual kickdown switch that will push the engine into second gear if the accelerator is floored for overtaking.

Power and performance

Even though it has the biggest passenger car engine in the world, the Cadillac is no hot-rod. It needs all of those cubic inches to drive the myriad

From the rear there are no gimmicks or fancy lighting arrangements. Lock to the trunk is under the badge on the Cadillac emblem.

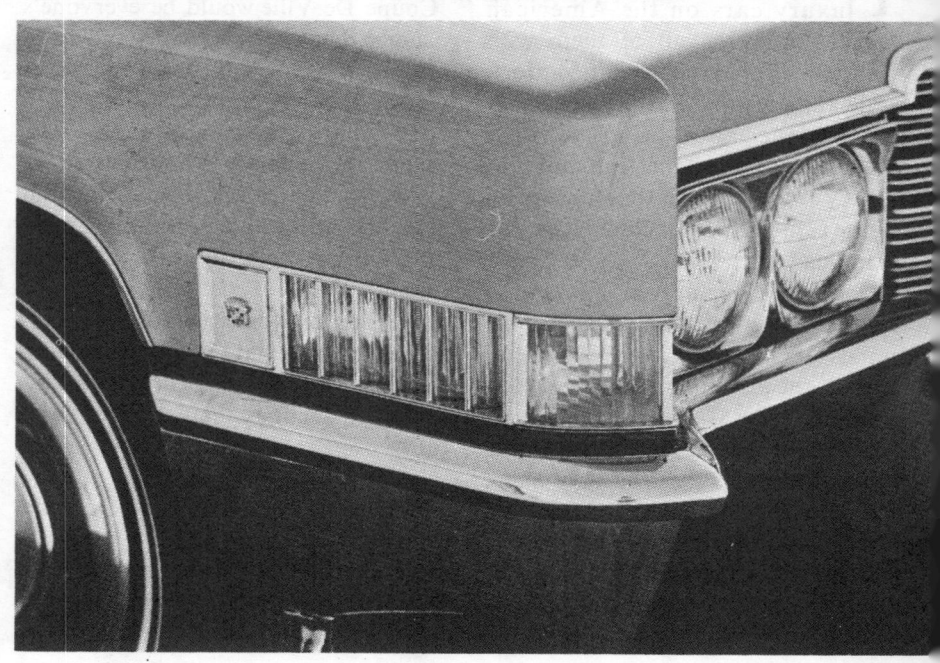

The thrusting fender tips incorporate wrap-around side lights to conform with safety regulations. Frontal projections may arouse criticism from safety purists.

Cadillac's smooth flanks feature a chrome protective strip to foil the parking lot hammer handed. Flowing lines reduce wind noise.

accessories and to haul its 4800 lbs. around at a respectable pace.

If asked to, however, the Coupe De Ville will move out at a rate calculated to surprise many of the other participants in the daily traffic light drag races.

We took the Cad to Orange County International Raceway and, driving it like few Cadillac owners ever would, returned an elapsed time for the quarter mile of 18.2 seconds. Terminal speed at the end of the quarter was 82.2 mph.

The times were taken using the transmission in the fully automatic manner and then with the driver making the shifts.

While using the box in the semi-automatic style resulted in a time of 17.7 seconds and a speed of 84.0 mph.

Checking the speedometer against the Orange County electronic equipment we found that it was actually doing 58.7 mph when the speedo' was indicating 60 mph.

The Coupe De Ville gets off the line with quite a lot of rearward weight transference (only to be expected with its soft suspension) and squealing wheelspin. As we said, however, few of the people likely to buy one would blast off from stop lights with tires ablaze. The Coupe De Ville has a more than adequate acceleration rate for normal driving without any wheelspinning drama and heroics.

On the freeways the Coupe De Ville is a pleasure to drive as far as power is concerned.

That huge V8 is chugging lazily away at an easy 70 mph cruising speed and can hardly be heard by the driver or passengers.

Should you need to overtake quickly, a stab on the accelerator pedal will kick the transmission down a gear and thrust you effortlessly past whatever you have to overtake.

The accent is on smoothness. There is no neck-breaking burst of acceleration, just a smooth surge of power and a glimpse of the speedo' needle swinging towards the fast end of the dial.

Roadability and handling

Where the Coupe De Ville does leave certain things to be desired is in the handling department. However, we have to bear in mind that the

Everything is immediately in front of the driver including the radio. The horn is in the steering wheel and only needs a squeeze to sound it.

Cadillac customer is unlikely to corner his Coupe De Ville in the Parnelli Jones or ROAD TEST manner. For the type of driver who is likely to buy it, the Coupe has safe and average handling though there is the inescapable fact that power steering and super-soft suspension do not make for a good handling car at speed.

So be warned. Should you see a little white-haired old lady approaching a 180° freeway off-ramp at 85 mph in her Coupe De Ville give her *lots* of room. She's going to need it to contend with the body lean and the understeer that are features of the Cadillac's behavior on fast corners.

Another control panel is in the driver's door for operating the windows and door locks. Three-speed wiper switch and screen washer button above. Outside rear view mirror adjustment is at the end of the arm rest.

Head restraints offer little obstruction to rear quarter viewing. The styling, however, leaves large blind spots on either side. Upholstery is in a rich brocade.

On the side of each front seat are found a trio of switches for position adjustment. The center switch moves the seat backward or forward. The outside two are for height and rake.

On the straight and level the ride in the Coupe De Ville is faultless. Smooth, comfortable and very little affected by crosswinds, it is a perfect freeway cruiser.

The only time you are likely to have any problems is if you have to make a sudden change of direction. Once again, the soft suspension and the massive bulk of the Cadillac mean that it does not take kindly to unheralded changes of plan. A quick swerve into a different lane, for example, brings with it a great transference of body weight and the car is somewhat slow in answering steering corrections.

The power steering itself is superb and has variable ratios that make it nice and easy for downtown traffic weaving and parking but stiffens up for fast highway driving.

All our comments about the rather imprecise handling boil down to one thing. It's a question of using 'horses for courses.' Use the Cadillac in the manner to which it is designed and it will give you no cause for alarm or complaint. Use it like a race car and it will give you plenty.

Brakes and safety

Safety is an aspect of car design that has received increasing attention for 1969 thanks to the stringent regulations imposed by the Federal government and the Cadillac has more than its share of safety innovations.

For example, the door frames have built-in safety bars that will withstand terrific impact so that if you are unfortunate enough to be hit from the side, the offending car will be kept from stuffing itself into your passenger compartment. Obviously a real direct impact at high speed would do you some damage but the safety bars would be more than useful if your car was struck a glancing blow by another, fast-moving vehicle.

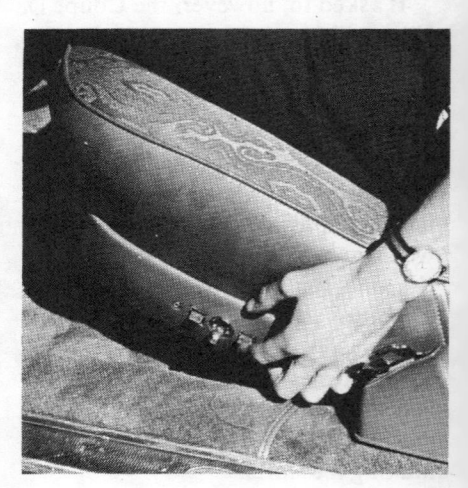

Lap and shoulder seat belts, deeply-padded dash panel, headrests, collapsible steering wheel ... all of the safety goodies are there plus a really good set of brakes.

The 1969 Cadillacs have discs on the front and large drum brakes at the rear and we found that our test model recorded a figure of 24/26 ft. per sec.^{2} on the decelerometer. This is indicative of a stop in 155 feet from 60 mph. In all but absolute panic stops the Coupe De Ville came to a halt straight and true.

What we didn't like about the braking was the too sudden power take-over and terrific transference of weight to the front end. As the brakes went on the long, heavy nose of the car dipped down. Then, as the car actually stopped, the nose snapped back up again. The sharp transference of weight frontwards and back again could really be felt by the passengers.

This is obviously another penalty one pays for the super-soft suspension.

The brake system is designed so that, should there be a leak in one half of the hydraulic system, the other half still provides some braking action.

A signal light in the instrument cluster warns the driver of any partial failure.

And naturally, like just about everything else on the Coupe De Ville the brakes are power-assisted.

Comfort and convenience

We have found a few points upon which we could criticize the Coupe De Ville. Now comes the part where criticism is extremely difficult, if not impossible, the areas of comfort and convenience.

Without exception, the Coupe De Ville just has to be one of the most comfortable cars on the road. The lush, deep seats are adjustable to virtually any leg position or back angle and give support just where it's needed . . . to the thighs, buttocks and small of the back.

Our test car had the all-electric setup by which the driver could do everything from adjust his seat, open his or all of the windows or lock the doors, simply by pressing one of the switches in the armrest of his door.

All the instruments are grouped closely together with easy-to-read dials. The steering wheel is fully adjustable to suit the driver's preference.

The stereo radio provides the best car music we have ever heard.

The climate control is highly effective and maintains a constant temperature pre-set by the driver. Controlling the interior temperature is just a matter of dialing whatever degree of heat you require (or cool, as the case may be) and letting the car's built-in brain do the rest of the work.

It's the same story with the cruise control, dial your number and the car does the rest. On long, long straight highways you can set the speed and stretch your legs . . . even drive standing on the seat if you are so inclined.

The lights dim automatically or manually, according to the driver's preference.

About all that can't be done by automation is the steering and braking, and these are power-assisted to make things easier.

Yes, from the point of view of comfort and convenience the only criticism that we can make of the Coupe De Ville is that so much is done for the driver that he begins to feel like a very minor part of the car's equipment. Rather a case of the car taking the driver for a ride instead of

With the standard front disc brakes, braking is good for such a heavy car. Stops were arrow straight without fuss.

the way things should be.

The Coupe De Ville must be the easiest car in the world to fall asleep in, whether you are moving or stationary.

If it weren't for that fantastic stereo we could have dozed off a number of times.

Summary

Summing up the attributes of a car like the Coupe De Ville means that a tester must try and look at it from several distinct viewpoints.

Whereas the huge, opulent bulk of the Cadillac effectively impresses a great many people it can have just the opposite effect on certain sober, conservative motorists, for example.

And those people who like transport in a fully-automated, self-thinking automobile are probably outweighed by those who like to actually *drive* a car and feel that they are the boss, or at least have some purpose in being at the controls.

However, the Cadillac *is* huge, it *does* make an impression on many people and it is *obviously* expensive. This latter fact, coupled with the fantastic comfort and luxury, is probably the main selling factor of the Coupe De Ville.

To the man stuck with his Frobisher six family sedan the Cadillac is

The 472 cubic inch V-8 engine developes 375 horsepower and 525 lb./ft. of torque. This hefty unit is the largest engine used in a passenger car anywhere in the world. It powers the big Coupe in absolute silence.

a symbol of wealth, something to be envied. And despite what anyone tries to tell you, impressing one's fellow men is still a great source of satisfaction to most people. The Coupe De Ville is a thing to impress with. ♠

A sealed cooling system means that you don't open the cap. Try it at your own risk. The system has to be topped up at the expansion tank.

Cadillac Coupe De Ville

Data in Brief

DIMENSIONS
Overall length (in.)	225.0
Width (in.)	79.9
Height (in.)	54.4
Track, front (in.)	63.0
Track, rear (in.)	63.0
Trunk capacity (cu. ft.)	00.0
Turning circle (ft.)	47.7
Wheelbase (in.)	129.5

WEIGHT, TIRES, BRAKES
Weight (lbs.)	4797
Tires	9.00 x 15
Brakes, front	disc
Brakes, rear	drum

ENGINE
Type	OHV V-8
Displacement (cu. in.)	472
Horsepower (Bhp)	375 at 4,400 rpm
Torque (ft/lbs)	525 at 3,000 rpm

SUSPENSION
Front	coil springs, wishbones
Rear	four-link, coil springs

PERFORMANCE
Standing ¼ mile (sec.)	17.7
Speed at end of ¼ mile (mph)	84.0
Passing (50-70 mph, sec.)	6.0
Braking from 60 mph (ft.)	155